Houghton Mifflin

Math Expressions

Volume 1

**Developed by
The Children's Math Worlds
Research Project**

PROJECT DIRECTOR AND AUTHOR

Dr. Karen C. Fuson

 This material is based upon work supported by the
National Science Foundation
under Grant Numbers
ESI-9816320, REC-9806020, and RED-935373.

Any opinions, findings, and conclusions or recommendations expressed in this
material are those of the author and do not necessarily reflect the views of the
National Science Foundation.

 HOUGHTON MIFFLIN   BOSTON

Teacher Reviewers

Kindergarten
Patricia Stroh Sugiyama
Wilmette, Illinois

Barbara Wahle
Evanston, Illinois

Grade 1
Sandra Budson
Newton, Massachusetts

Janet Pecci
Chicago, Illinois

Megan Rees
Chicago, Illinois

Grade 2
Molly Dunn
Danvers, Massachusetts

Agnes Lesnick
Hillside, Illinois

Rita Soto
Chicago, Illinois

Grade 3
Jane Curran
Honesdale, Pennsylvania

Sandra Tucker
Chicago, Illinois

Grade 4
Sara Stoneberg Llibre
Chicago, Illinois

Sheri Roedel
Chicago, Illinois

Grade 5
Todd Atler
Chicago, Illinois

Leah Barry
Norfolk, Massachusetts

Special Thanks

Special thanks to the many teachers, students, parents, principals, writers, researchers, and work-study students who participated in the Children's Math Worlds Research Project over the years.

Credits

Cover art: (tiger) © Juniors Bildarchiv/Alamy Images. (whale) © Francois Gohier/Photo Researchers, Inc. (grass) © Corel Stock Photo Library. (tape) © Eyewire.

Illustrative art: Robin Boyer/Deborah Wolfe, LTD
Technical art: Nesbitt Graphics, Inc.
Photos: Nesbitt Graphics, Inc.

Printed in the U.S.A.

ISBN-13: 978-0-618-50980-5
ISBN-10: 0-618-50980-1

4 5 6 7 8 9 KDL 11 10 09 08 07

VOLUME 1 CONTENTS

* This lesson consists only of activities from the Teacher's Guide.

* This lesson consists only of activities from the Teacher's Guide.

VOLUME 1 CONTENTS

* This lesson consists only of activities from the Teacher's Guide.

Class Activity

Name _____

Vocabulary

story problems   altogether
in all

▶ **Solve and Discuss Story Problems**

Solve the **story problems**.

Show your work.

1. Andrew has 3 balloons. Erin has 6. How many do they have **altogether**?

   ☐ _____
        label

balloon

2. There are 5 boys and some girls on the bus. There are 9 children on the bus. How many girls are on the bus?

   ☐ _____
        label

bus

3. There are 8 bananas and some apples. There are 12 pieces of fruit **in all**. How many apples are there?

   ☐ _____
        label

fruit

4. Ashley keeps 6 stuffed toys on the shelf. She has some on her bed. Altogether she has 15 stuffed toys. How many are on her bed?

   ☐ _____
        label

stuffed toy

5. **On the Back** Write your own story problem that asks, "How many in all?" Then solve the problem.

Name _____

_____

_____

_____

_____

_____

_____

_____

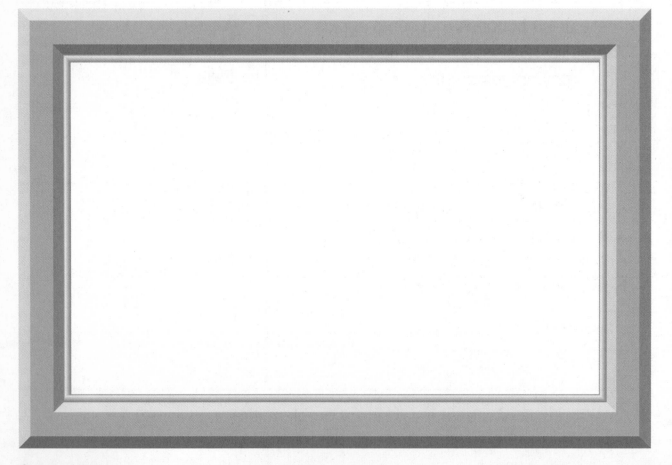

Introduce Stories and Drawings

Dear Family,

Your child is learning math in a new program called *Math Expressions* which links mathematical ideas to a child's everyday experiences. This helps children understand math better.

In this program, your child will learn math and have fun by

- working with objects and making drawings of math situations.
- listening to and working with other children and sharing ways to solve problems.
- writing and solving problems and connecting math to daily life.
- helping classmates learn.

Your child will have homework almost every day. He or she needs a Homework Helper. The helper may be anyone—a family member, an older brother or sister, a neighbor, or a friend. Set aside a definite time for homework and provide your child with a quiet place to work where there is no TV or radio. Encourage your child to talk about what is happening in math class. If your child is having problems with math, please talk to me to see how you might help.

Please cut out, fill out, and return the bottom part of this letter.

Thank you. You are very important to your child's learning.

Sincerely,
Your child's teacher

- -

My child _____ will have
(child's name)

_____ as a Homework Helper.
(name of homework helper)

This person is my child's _____.
(relationship to child)

_____
Signature of parent or guardian

Carta a la familia

Estimada familia:

Su niño está aprendiendo matemáticas con un programa innovador llamado *Math Expressions,* que relaciona conceptos matemáticos abstractos con la experiencia diaria de los niños. Esto ayuda a los niños a entender mejor las matemáticas.

Con este programa, su niño va a aprender matemáticas y se divertirá mientras

- trabaja con objetos y hace dibujos de situaciones matemáticas.
- escucha y trabaja con otros estudiantes y comparte con ellos estrategias para resolver problemas.
- escribe y resuelve problemas, y relaciona las matemáticas con la vida diaria.
- ayuda a sus compañeros de clase a aprender.

Su niño tendrá tarea casi todos los días y necesitrá a una persona que lo ayude con la tarea. Esa persona puede ser, usted, un hermano mayor, un vecino o un amigo. Establezca una hora para la tarea y ofrezca a su niño un lugar tranquilo donde trabajar (sin televisión o radio). Anime a su niño a comentar lo que está aprendiendo en la clase de matemáticas. Si él tiene problemas con las matemáticas, hable por favor con el maestro para ver cómo usted puede ayudar.

Por favor escriba la siguiente información y devuelva este formulario al maestro.

Muchas gracias. Usted es imprescindible en el aprendizaje de su niño.

Atentamente,
El maestro de su niño

La persona que ayudará a mi niño _____ es
(nombre del niño)

_____. Esta persona es
(nombre de la persona)

_____ de mi niño.
(relación con el niño)

_____
Su firma

Class Activity

▶ **Solve and Discuss Story Problems**

Solve the **story problems**. You may want to make a **matching drawing**.

Show your work.

1. Roberto has 6 coins in his collection. Cass has 10 in hers. How many more coins does Cass have than Roberto?

   ☐ _____
         label

coin

2. 13 bears live in a cave. 7 of them went out. How many bears are in the cave?

   ☐ _____
         label

cave

3. Ivan has won 9 ribbons for running. Dan has won 5. How many fewer ribbons does Dan have than Ivan?

   ☐ _____
         label

ribbon

4. Zeke bought 4 toys. Laura bought 7. How many more toys must Zeke buy to have as many as Laura?

   ☐ _____
         label

toy

5. **On the Back** Write your own story problem about toys. Then solve the problem.

Name _____

_____

_____

_____

_____

_____

_____

_____

_____

_____

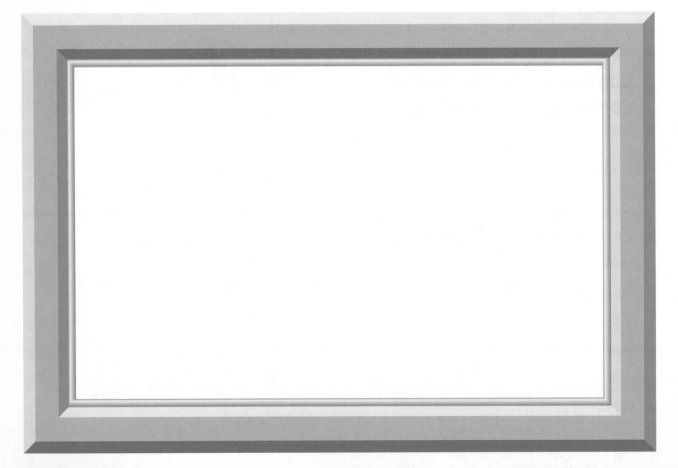

Practice with Stories and Drawings

Class Activity

Name _____

▶ **Solve and Discuss**

Solve the **story problems**.

Show your work.

1. Dawn ate 5 orange slices. Kim ate 8 slices. How many fewer orange slices did Dawn eat than Kim?

   ☐ _____

   label

orange slice

2. Alice had 16 apples. Her friends ate 7. How many apples are left?

   ☐ _____

   label

apple

3. Riley saw 4 robins on the nature trail and some blue jays on the way home. Altogether he saw 10 birds. How many blue jays did he see?

   ☐ _____

   label

birds

4. Dillon made 6 clay pots in the morning. He made some more that afternoon. Altogether Dillon made 14 clay pots. How many did he make in the afternoon?

   ☐ _____

   label

clay pot

Extra Practice

Name _____

Add or subtract.

If the answer is 3, color YELLOW   If the answer is 4, color RED

If the answer is 5, color GREEN   If the answer is 6, color BLUE

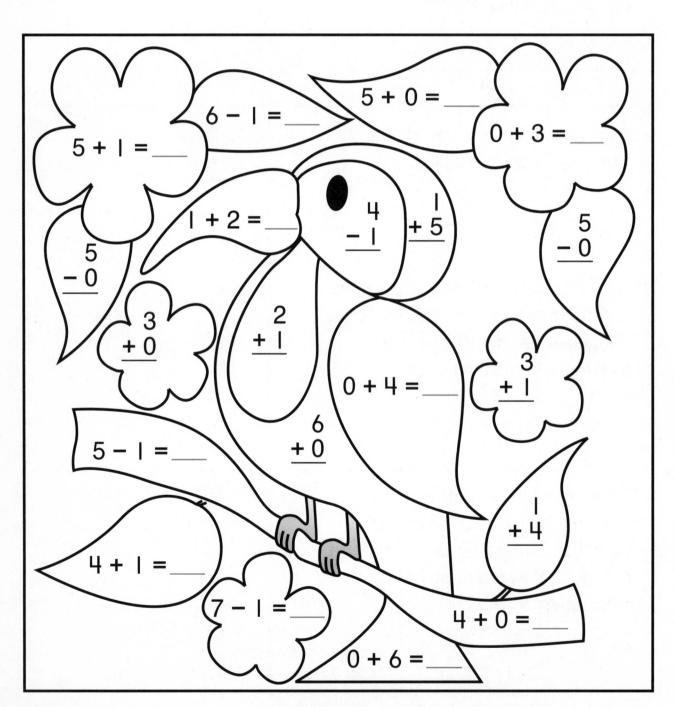

$5 + 1 =$ ___

$6 - 1 =$ ___

$5 + 0 =$ ___

$0 + 3 =$ ___

$1 + 2 =$ ___

$\begin{array}{r} 4 \\ -1 \\ \hline \end{array}$

$\begin{array}{r} 1 \\ +5 \\ \hline \end{array}$

$\begin{array}{r} 5 \\ -0 \\ \hline \end{array}$

$\begin{array}{r} 5 \\ -0 \\ \hline \end{array}$

$\begin{array}{r} 3 \\ +0 \\ \hline \end{array}$

$\begin{array}{r} 2 \\ +1 \\ \hline \end{array}$

$0 + 4 =$ ___

$\begin{array}{r} 3 \\ +1 \\ \hline \end{array}$

$5 - 1 =$ ___

$\begin{array}{r} 6 \\ +0 \\ \hline \end{array}$

$\begin{array}{r} 1 \\ +4 \\ \hline \end{array}$

$4 + 1 =$ ___

$7 - 1 =$ ___

$4 + 0 =$ ___

$0 + 6 =$ ___

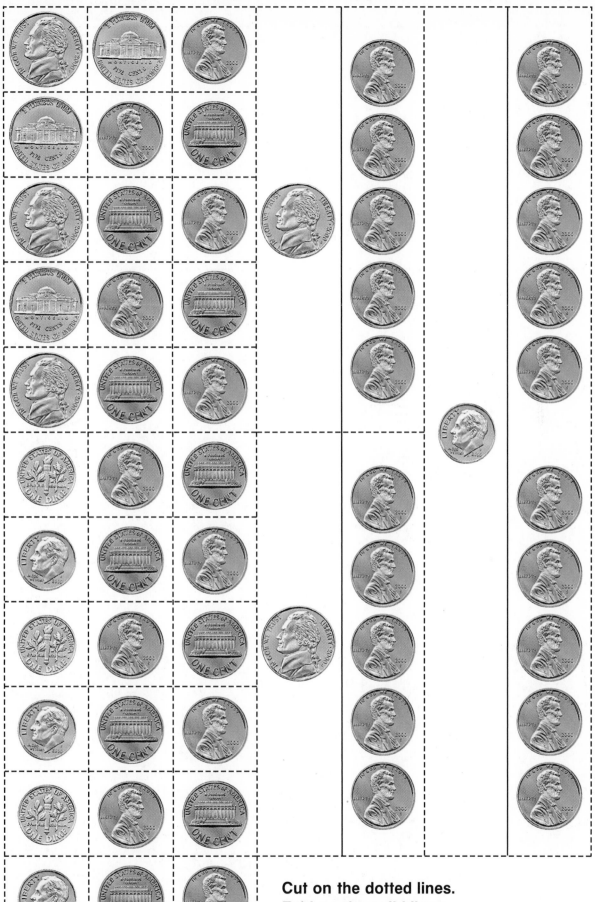

Cut on the dotted lines.
Fold on the solid lines.

Coin Strips

1	2	10	20
1	2	1 0	2 0

3	4	30	40
3	4	3 0	4 0

5	6	50	60
5	6	5 0	6 0

7	8	70	80
7	8	7 0	8 0

9	90	100
9	9 0	1 0 0

Secret Code Cards (1–100)

200	300
2 0 0	3 0 0

400	500
4 0 0	5 0 0

600	700
6 0 0	7 0 0

800	900
8 0 0	9 0 0

1000
1 0 0 0

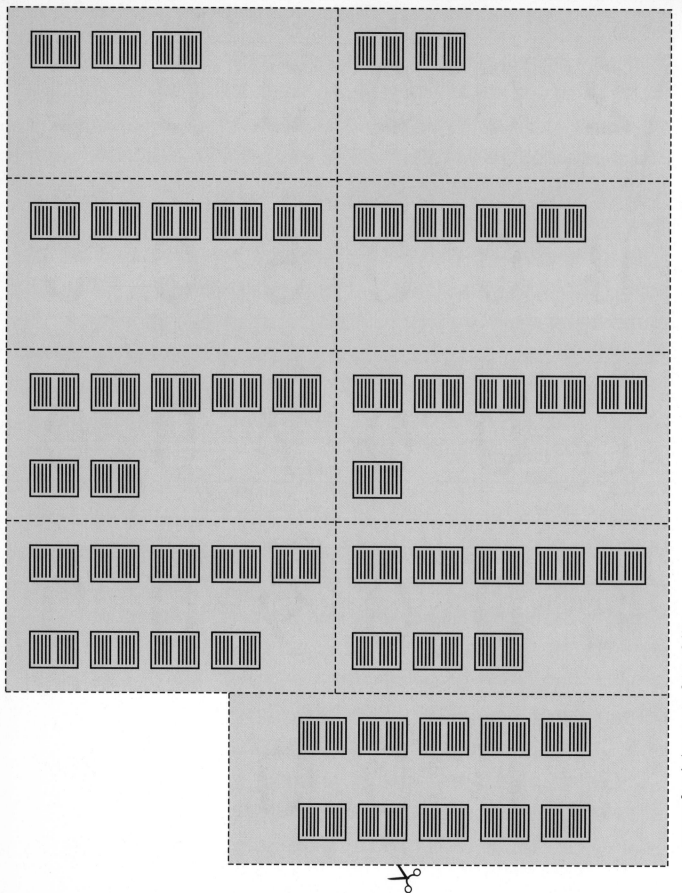

Secret Code Cards (200–1000)

Class Activity

Name _____

▶ **Discuss Patterns**

Discuss the **patterns** you see.

1 ·	one	11	eleven
2 ··	two	12	twelve
3 ···	three	13	thirteen
4 ····	four	14	fourteen
5 ·····	five	15	fifteen
6 :····	six	16	sixteen
7 ::···	seven	17	seventeen
8 :::··	eight	18	eighteen
9 ::::·	nine	19	nineteen
10	ten	20	twenty

Class Activity

Vocabulary

patterns

▶ Word Names and Patterns

Write the word name for each number.

Word Names	
one	eleven
two	twelve
three	thirteen
four	fourteen
five	fifteen
six	sixteen
seven	seventeen
eight	eighteen
nine	nineteen
ten	twenty

1. 16 _____

2. 10 _____

3. 7 _____

4. 19 _____

5. 13 _____

6. 11 _____

Draw a line to match each word name with the correct number.

7. fifteen   11

8. seventeen   18

9. eleven   12

10. twenty   15

11. eight   17

12. eighteen   8

13. twelve   20

14. **Look for a Pattern** What **patterns** do you see in the word names? Use the Word Names box to help you.

_____

_____

_____

Teens, Tens, and Dimes

Dear Family,

In this unit your child will explore smaller numbers that are "hiding" inside a larger number. The activities will help your child master addition and subtraction.

To make the ideas clearer, *Math Expressions* uses some special words and materials.

- **Break-Apart** We can "break apart" the larger number to get two smaller numbers. Your child is using objects and drawings to explore the different ways to break apart a number. For example, 6 can break apart as: 1 + 5, 2 + 4, 3 + 3.

- **Partners** Partners of a number are any two smaller numbers that together make the total. For example, 6 has these partners: 1 and 5, 2 and 4, 3 and 3.

- **Switch the Partners** The partners can be switched and the total stays the same. For example, 1 + 5 = 6 and 5 + 1 = 6 .

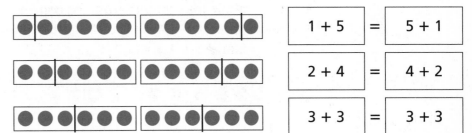

Children will also be asked to fill in **Partner Houses**. These drawings show the numbers hiding inside the larger number.

Please call if you need practice materials. Thank you.

Sincerely,
Your child's teacher

Estimada familia:

En esta unidad su niño estudiará a los números más pequeños que "se esconden" dentro de un número más grande. Las actividades ayudarán a su niño a dominar la suma y la resta.

Para presentar los conceptos de manera más clara, *Math Expressions* usa palabras y materiales especiales.

- **Separar** Podemos "separar" el número más grande para obtener dos números más pequeños. Su niño está usando objetos y dibujos para ver las diferentes maneras de separar un número. Por ejemplo, el 6 se puede separar como 1 + 5, 2 + 4, 3 + 3.

- **Compañeros** Los compañeros o partes de un número son todos los pares de números más pequeños que juntos pueden formar el total. Por ejemplo, el 6 tiene estos compañeros: 1 y 5, 2 y 4, 3 y 3.

- **Intercambiar los compañeros** Los compañeros se pueden intercambiar y el total seguirá siendo el mismo. Por ejemplo, 1 + 5 = 6 and 5 + 1 = 6 .

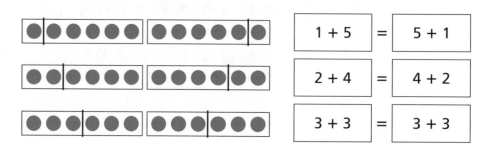

También se les pedirá a los niños que llenen **Casas de compañeros**. Estos dibujos muestran los números que están escondidos en el número más grande.

Por favor comuníquese conmigo si necesita materiales para practicar. Gracias.

Atentamente,
El maestro de su niño

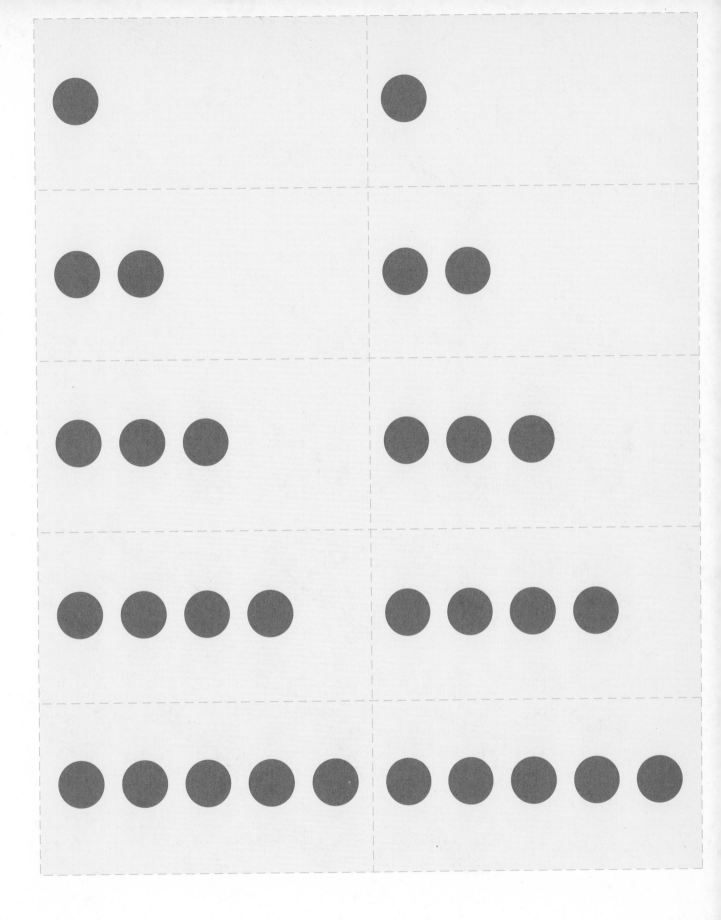

Dot Cards

Going Further

▶ *Making Totals* **Game**

You need: Dot Cards for numbers 1–5 from Student
Activity Book page 19

How to play:

1. Play with a classmate. Shuffle the cards and deal three
to each player.

2. Each player chooses two of the three cards and finds
the total.

3. Players record the partners for the total in the correct
space on their sheet. Then they put the cards back in
the deck and reshuffle.

4. The game continues until one player has found
partners for all totals 2–10.

Write the partners you used for each total.

Total of 2	**Total of 3**	**Total of 4**
_____ and _____	_____ and _____	_____ and _____
Total of 5	**Total of 6**	**Total of 7**
_____ and _____	_____ and _____	_____ and _____
Total of 8	**Total of 9**	**Total of 10**
_____ and _____	_____ and _____	_____ and _____

Partners in Break-Aparts

Class Activity

Name _____

Vocabulary
count on

▶ **Count On to Find the Total**   6 + 3 = $\boxed{9}$

6

6   ∙∙∙ | Already **6** $\overset{8\ 9}{\underset{7}{}}$ | Already **6** ∙∙∙ $\overset{}{7\ 8\ 9}$

I pretend I already counted 6. So 7, 8, 9.

Count on to find the total.

1. 5 + 3 = ☐   3 + 9 = ☐   4 + 9 = ☐

2. 4 + 3 = ☐   4 + 8 = ☐   2 + 6 = ☐

3. 9 + 4 = ☐   2 + 9 = ☐   8 + 5 = ☐

4. 8 + 6 = ☐   4 + 6 = ☐   3 + 6 = ☐

5. 7 + 2 = ☐   5 + 9 = ☐   4 + 5 = ☐

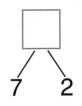

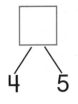

6. **Explain Your Thinking** Explain how to count on to find the total of 2 + 9. What is the total?

_____

_____

Name _____

Going Further

▶ Introduce Function Tables

Follow the rule to complete each table.

1.

Add 3	
0	
1	
2	
3	

2.

Subtract 1	
10	
9	
8	
7	

3.

Add 5	
4	
5	
6	
7	

Find the rule. Then complete each table.

4.

Add 2	
3	
4	
5	
6	

5.

Add 4	
7	
8	
9	
10	

6.

Add 9	
8	
7	
6	
5	

7. **Create Your Own** Make your own table. Write a rule and fill in the numbers in the first column of the table. Have a partner follow the rule and finish the table.

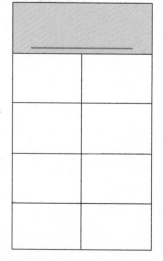

Count On to Find the Total

Dear Family,

In *Math Expressions,* we teach children a faster method for addition. Instead of **counting all** the objects to find the total, children can pretend that they already counted one number and just **count on** from it to the total. Children should understand that the last number they say is the total.

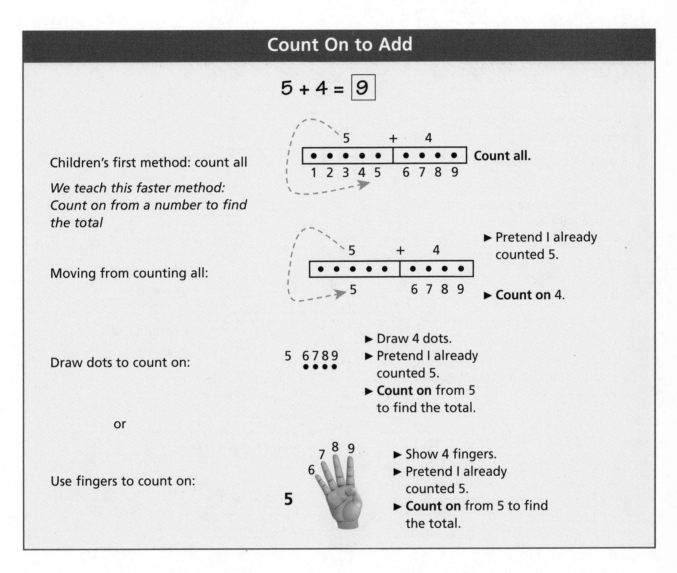

Count On to Add

$$5 + 4 = \boxed{9}$$

Children's first method: count all

We teach this faster method: Count on from a number to find the total

5 + 4

1 2 3 4 5   6 7 8 9   **Count all.**

Moving from counting all:

5 + 4

5   6 7 8 9

▶ Pretend I already counted 5.

▶ **Count on** 4.

Draw dots to count on:

5 6789

▶ Draw 4 dots.
▶ Pretend I already counted 5.
▶ **Count on** from 5 to find the total.

or

Use fingers to count on:

7 8 9
6
5

▶ Show 4 fingers.
▶ Pretend I already counted 5.
▶ **Count on** from 5 to find the total.

Please call if you have any questions or comments.

Sincerely,
Your child's teacher

Estimada familia:

Con *Math Expressions,* les enseñamos a los niños un método de suma más rápido. En vez de **contar todos** los objetos para hallar el total, ellos imaginan que ya han contado un número y sólo **cuentan hacia adelante** desde ese número, hasta llegar al total. Los niños deben comprender que el total es el último número que dicen.

Contar hacia adelante para sumar

$$5 + 4 = \boxed{9}$$

Primer método usado por los niños: Contar todo

Enseñamos este método más rápido:

Contar hacia adelante desde un número para hallar el total

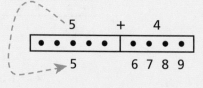

5 + 4

1 2 3 4 5 6 7 8 9 **Contar todo**

Sin contar todo:

5 + 4

5 6 7 8 9

► Imaginar que ya conté 5

► **Contar hacia adelante 4**

Dibujar puntos para contar hacia adelante:

5 6789

► Dibujar 4 puntos.
► Imaginar que ya conté 5.
► **Contar hacia adelante** desde 5 para hallar el total.

o

Usar los dedos para contar hacia adelante:

7 8 9
6
5

► Mostrar 4 dedos.
► Imaginar que ya conté 5.
► **Contar hacia adelante** desde 5 para hallar el total.

Si tiene alguna pregunta o comentario, por favor comuníquese conmigo.

Atentamente,
El maestro de su niño

Count On to Find the Partner

Class Activity

Name

Vocabulary

count on

partner

▶ **Relate Addition and Subtraction**

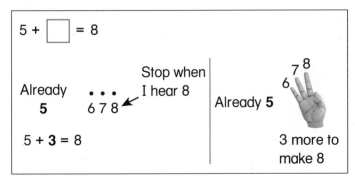

$5 + \boxed{} = 8$

Already **5**

Stop when I hear 8

$\cdots$

6 7 8

$5 + 3 = 8$

Already **5**

3 more to make 8

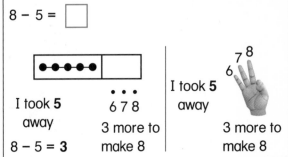

$8 - 5 = \boxed{}$

I took **5** away

$8 - 5 = 3$

$\cdots$

6 7 8

3 more to make 8

I took **5** away

3 more to make 8

Count on to find the **partner**.

1. $6 + \boxed{} = 9$ $\qquad$ $9 - 6 = \boxed{}$ $\qquad$ $6 + \boxed{} = 10$

2. $7 + \boxed{} = 10$ $\qquad$ $10 - 8 = \boxed{}$ $\qquad$ $3 + \boxed{} = 12$

3. $5 + \boxed{} = 9$ $\qquad$ $13 - 9 = \boxed{}$ $\qquad$ $4 + \boxed{} = 9$

4. $9 + \boxed{} = 14$ $\qquad$ $8 - 3 = \boxed{}$ $\qquad$ $7 + \boxed{} = 11$

5. $6 + \boxed{} = 8$ $\qquad$ $13 - 9 = \boxed{}$ $\qquad$ $10 - \boxed{} = 3$

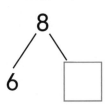

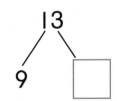

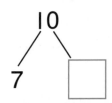

6. Make a Proof Drawing for $11 - 7 = \boxed{}$.

Going Further

▶ **Use Logical Reasoning**

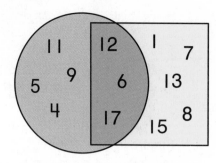

Use logical reasoning to solve.

1. I am a number inside the circle.
   I am the total of two other numbers inside the circle.
   I am greater than 10. What number am I? _____

2. I am a number inside the square.
   I am the total of two numbers outside the circle.
   I am less than 10. What number am I? _____

3. I am a number inside **both** the circle and the square.
   I am greater than 10. I am less than 15.
   What number am I? _____

4. I am a number outside the square.
   I am a total of two other numbers outside the square.
   What number am I? _____

5. **Write Your Own** Write your own number riddle for
   the picture. Make sure you can solve it.

   _____

   _____

   _____

Dear Family,

Your child has learned to solve addition problems by counting on to find the total. Now your child will use **partner counting on** to solve "mystery" addition problems (5 + ☐ = 9) and subtraction problems (9 − 5 = ☐).

Partner Counting On

Mystery Addition

Partner Counting On Children count on from the partner they know to the total in order to find the unknown partner. The answer is how many numbers they counted on.

$$5 + \square = 9$$

• • • •

Already 5   6 7 8 9   Stop when I hear 9.

I count 4 more to make 9 so 4 is the unknown partner. So, 5 + 4 = 9.

Subtraction

Take Away For subtraction, children's first method is take away, but you have to draw all 9 dots.

Partner Counting On Counting on from 5 to 9 is faster and easier: You only make dots for the difference.

$$9 - 5 = \square$$

Draw 9 dots. Cross out 5.

| • • • • • | • • • • |

| 5 | • • • • |
         6 7 8 9

Already took away 5.   Stop when I hear 9. 4 more to make 9. So, 9 − 5 = 4.

Finger Method Some children may choose to use their fingers to count on from the partner to the total.

Thank you for helping your child learn mathematics.

Sincerely,
Your child's teacher

Carta a la familia

Estimada familia:

Su niño ha aprendido a sumar y a hallar el total contando hacia adelante. Ahora su niño o niña usará el método de **contar compañeros hacia adelante** para sumas (5 + ☐ = 9) y restas (9 − 5 = ☐) con un "número misterioso".

Contar hacia adelante con compañeros

Suma con un compañero desconocido

Contar compañeros hacia adelante
Para poder hallar el compañero desconocido, los niños cuentan hacia adelante desde el número que conocen hasta el total. La respuesta será la cantidad de números que hayan contado hacia adelante.

$5 + ☐ = 9$

• • • •

Ya tengo 5.   6 7 8 9   Paro cuando escucho el 9.

Para llegar a 9 cuento 4 más, entonces 4 es el compañero desconocido. Así, $5 + \boxed{4} = 9$

Resta

Quitar Para restar, el primer método que usan los niños es el de quitar, pero hay que dibujar los 9 puntos.

$9 − 5 = ☐$

Dibujo 9 puntos. Tacho 5.

6 7 8 9

Contar compañeros hacia adelante
Contar hacia adelante del 5 al 9 es más rápido y más fácil. Sólo se marcan los puntos que indiquen la diferencia.

Ya quité 5.   Paro cuando escucho 9. 4 más para llegar a 9. Entonces, $9 − 5 = \boxed{4}$

Contar con los dedos Algunos niños pueden preferir contar hacia adelante con los dedos desde el compañero hasta el total.

Gracias por ayudar a su niño a aprender matemáticas.

Atentamente,
El maestro de su niño

Name _____

Class Activity

▶ Practice Finding Totals and Partners

Are we looking for a **partner** or **total**?
Ring the P or the T for each column.
Put a ﹏﹏ under each partner.

	P or T ↓	P or T ↓	P or T ↓
1.	$5 + 3 = \square$	$5 + \square = 8$	$8 - 5 = \square$
2.	$4 + 8 = \square$	$4 + \square = 12$	$12 - 4 = \square$
3.	$7 + 3 = \square$	$7 + \square = 10$	$10 - 7 = \square$
4.	$6 + 8 = \square$	$6 + \square = 14$	$14 - 6 = \square$
5.	$5 + 4 = \square$	$5 + \square = 9$	$9 - 5 = \square$
6.	$7 + 6 = \square$	$7 + \square = 13$	$13 - 7 = \square$
7.	$6 + 4 = \square$	$6 + \square = 10$	$10 - 6 = \square$

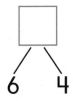

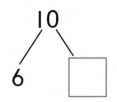

Going Further

▶ **Match the Equation to the Story Problem**

Draw a line to match the story problem to
an equation. Then solve the equation.
Write the answer.

1. Laurie had 2 crayons. Then she got
   some more. Now she has 5. How many
   more did Laurie get?

   ☐
   _____
   label

2. Laurie had 5 crayons. Then she gave 2
   away. How many does Laurie have left?

   ☐
   _____
   label

3. Laurie had some crayons. Then she got
   2 more. Now she has 5. How many did
   Laurie have to start?

   ☐
   _____
   label

4. Laurie had 5 crayons. Then she gave
   some away. Now she has 2 left. How
   many did Laurie give away?

   ☐
   _____
   label

$2 + \boxed{} = 5$

$\boxed{} + 2 = 5$

$5 - \boxed{} = 2$

$5 - 2 = \boxed{}$

$\boxed{} - 2 = 5$

Relate Addition and Subtraction

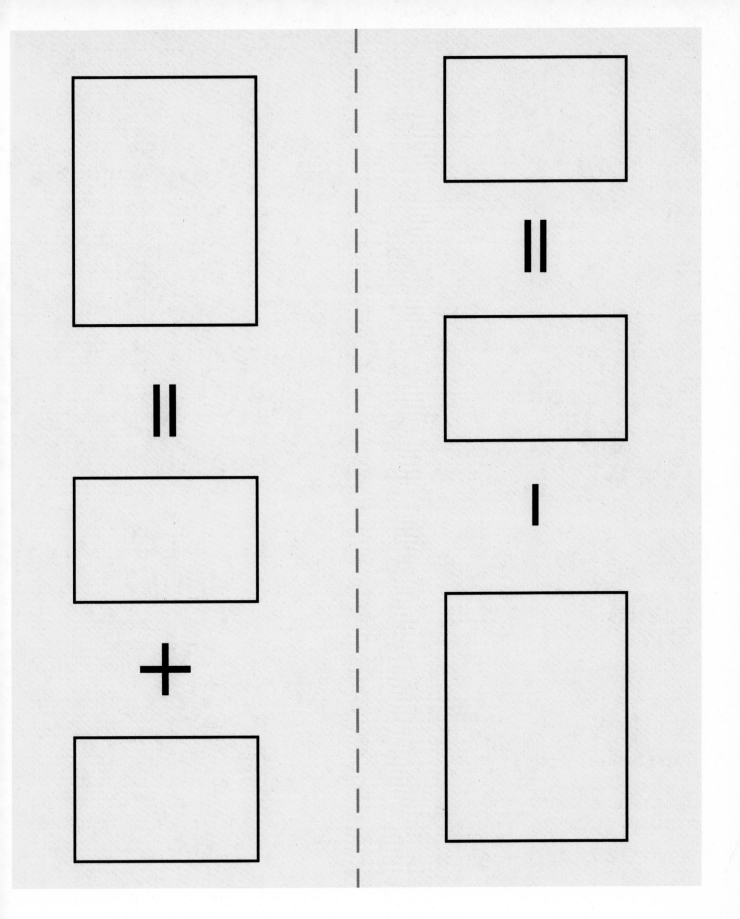

Relate Addition and Subtraction

Math Mountain Cards — addition facts (triangular flash cards; some printed inverted for cut-out/fold)

0 + 1   0 + 3   0 + 5

0   2   4   6

1   3   5

0 + 0   0 + 2   0 + 4   0 + 6

7 + 0   6 + 0   2 + 1   4 + 1

8   2   4

7   6   3   5

0 + 8   1 + 1   1 + 3

1 + 1   8 + 1   2 + 2   3 + 2

6   8   10   5

7   6   4

1 + 5   1 + 7   1 + 9   3 + 2

4 + 3   9 + 2   8 + 2   3 + 3

7   9   10

6   8   10   9

5 + 2   7 + 2   5 + 5

Relate Addition and Subtraction–Teen Totals

5 + 3   7 + 3   4 + 3   5 + 4
  7   9   10   8

  − 8   − 10   − 6
4 + 3   6 + 3   4 + 6   4 + 4

6 + 3   4 + 7   4 + 7   5 + 9   6 + 9
  11   12   11

  − 12   − 11   − 13   − 11
  8 + 3   4 + 8   9 + 2

5 + 8   6 + 8   8 + 8   6 + 9
  12   14   13   15

  − 13   − 12   − 14
5 + 7   5 + 9   7 + 6   9 + 6

7 + 7   6 + 7   6 + 9   8 + 9
  15   16   18

  − 14   − 16   − 17
8 + 7   8 + 8   9 + 9

Relate Addition and Subtraction–Teen Totals

Dear Family,

Your child is exploring addition and subtraction equations with Math Mountain Cards. The cards have a large number at the top and two smaller numbers at the bottom. From the cards, children can see that two smaller numbers can be added together to make a large number. They can also see that a large number can be broken apart into two smaller numbers.

Children will write addition and subtraction equations that they can make from the cards, as shown in the example. The two partners, 5 and 3, can be added to make the total, 8. They can be switched (3 and 5) and still make 8.

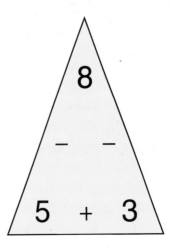

5 + 3 = 8	8 = 5 + 3
3 + 5 = 8	8 = 3 + 5
8 − 5 = 3	3 = 8 − 5
8 − 3 = 5	5 = 8 − 3

Students see and write all 8 equations. It is important for understanding algebra that they see equations with only one number on the left.

Please call if you need practice materials. Thank you for helping your child learn about the relationship between addition and subtraction.

Sincerely,
Your child's teacher

Estimada familia:

Su niño está aprendiendo ecuaciones de suma y resta usando las tarjetas *Math Mountain.* Las tarjetas tienen un número grande en la parte superior y dos números más pequeños en la parte inferior. En las tarjetas los niños pueden ver que se puede sumar dos números más pequeños para obtener un número más grande. También pueden ver que un número grande se puede separar en dos números más pequeños.

Los niños escribirán ecuaciones de suma y resta que puedan hacer a partir de las tarjetas, según se muestra en el ejemplo. Se puede sumar los dos compañeros, 5 y 3, para obtener el total, 8. También se puede intercambiar (3 y 5) y todavía obtener 8.

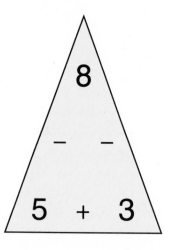

5 + 3 = 8	8 = 5 + 3
3 + 5 = 8	8 = 3 + 5
8 − 5 = 3	3 = 8 − 5
8 − 3 = 5	5 = 8 − 3

Los estudiantes ven y escriben las 8 ecuaciones. Para la comprensión de álgebra es importante que vean ecuaciones con on solo número a la izquierda.

Por favor comuníquese conmigo si necesita materiales para practicar. Gracias por ayudar a su niño a aprender la relación entre suma y resta.

Atentamente,
El maestro de su niño

Relate Addition and Subtraction–Teen Totals

Parachute Drop

$5 + 3 = \boxed{8}$ $5 + \boxed{3} = 8$ $8 - 5 = \boxed{3}$

$6 + 2 = \boxed{8}$ $6 + \boxed{2} = 8$ $8 - 6 = \boxed{2}$

$4 + 5 = \boxed{9}$ $4 + \boxed{5} = 9$ $9 - 4 = \boxed{5}$

$3 + 6 = \boxed{9}$ $3 + \boxed{6} = 9$ $9 - 3 = \boxed{6}$

$2 + 4 = \boxed{6}$ $2 + \boxed{4} = 6$ $6 - 2 = \boxed{4}$

$6 + 4 = \boxed{10}$ $6 + \boxed{4} = 10$ $10 - 6 = \boxed{4}$

$4 + 3 = \boxed{7}$ $4 + \boxed{3} = 7$ $7 - 4 = \boxed{3}$

$3 + 7 = \boxed{10}$ $3 + \boxed{7} = 10$ $10 - 3 = \boxed{7}$

$8 + 2 = \boxed{10}$ $8 + \boxed{2} = 10$ $10 - 8 = \boxed{2}$

$3 + 2 = \boxed{5}$ $3 + \boxed{2} = 5$ $5 - 2 = \boxed{3}$

$4 + 4 = \boxed{8}$ $4 + \boxed{4} = 8$ $8 - 4 = \boxed{4}$

Equations from Math Mountains

Class Activity

Name _____

Vocabulary

equations
Math Mountain
partners

▶ **Math Mountain Equations**

Find all of the **equations** for each **Math Mountain**.
Draw squiggles under the **partners**.

1. $9 + 3 = 12$

$12 = 9 + 3$

_____

_____

_____

_____

_____

_____

2. $6 + 8 = 14$

$14 = 6 + 8$

_____

_____

_____

_____

_____

_____

➡ **3. On the Back** Write and solve a story problem
for one of the equations above.

Name _____

_____

_____

_____

_____

_____

_____

_____

_____

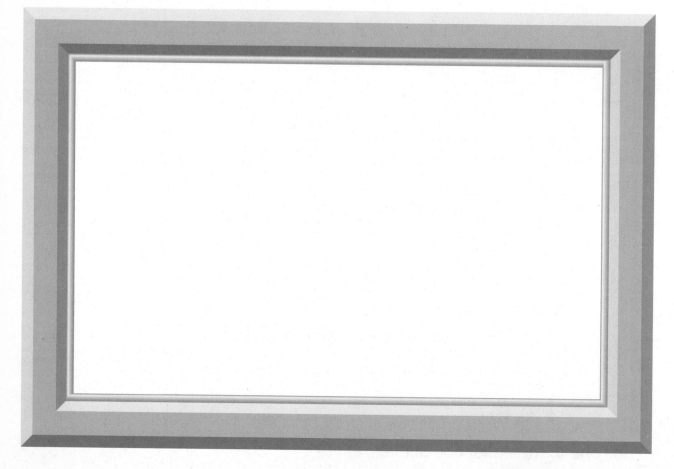

Equations from Math Mountains

Class Activity

▶ **Match Problems and Equations**

Match the story problems with the equations.

1. Janie found 8 shells. Her sister found 4 shells. How many shells did Janie and her sister find altogether?

$8 + \square = 12$

2. There are 12 boys and girls in the park. 4 of the children are girls. How many boys are in the park?

$8 + 4 = \square$

3. Sovann had 8 pennies. Then he found some more pennies. Sovann has 12 pennies in all. How many pennies did Sovann find?

$\square + 4 = 12$

4. Aliya has 4 pens. She bought some at the store. Aliya now has 8 pens. How many pens did she buy at the store?

$4 + \square = 8$

5. Julie ran some laps and then ran 4 more laps for a total of 12 laps. How many laps did she run in the beginning?

$12 = 4 + \square$

➡ 6. **On the Back** Write and solve a story problem for

$\square - 7 = 9.$

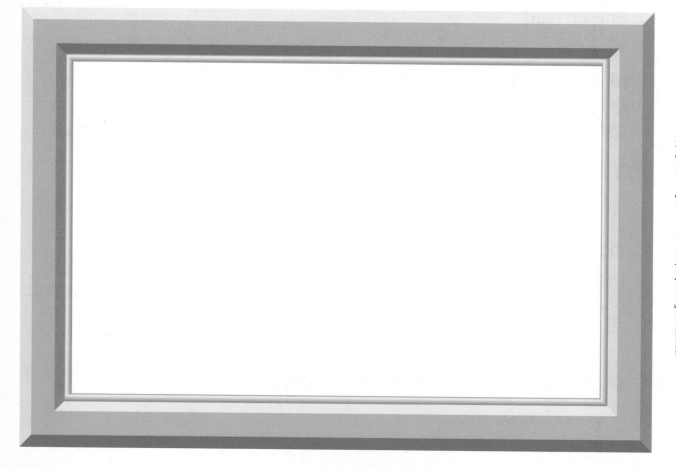

Stories from Math Mountains

Class Activity

▶ **Add Three Numbers**

You can add in three different ways. $5 + 4 + 3 = \boxed{}$

$9 \quad + 3$	$5 + \quad 7$	$8 + 4$
$5 + 4 + 3 = \boxed{12}$	$5 + 4 + 3 = \boxed{12}$	$5 + 4 + 3 = \boxed{12}$

Choose what to add first. Then find the **teen total**.

1. $4 + 2 + 5 = \boxed{}$ $\quad$ $5 + 4 + 5 = \boxed{}$ $\quad$ $2 + 6 + 4 = \boxed{}$

2. $6 + 3 + 4 = \boxed{}$ $\quad$ $4 + 5 + 3 = \boxed{}$ $\quad$ $2 + 7 + 2 = \boxed{}$

3. $9 + 5 + 2 = \boxed{}$ $\quad$ $5 + 8 + 2 = \boxed{}$ $\quad$ $6 + 9 + 4 = \boxed{}$

4. $3 + 6 + 3 = \boxed{}$ $\quad$ $8 + 2 + 7 = \boxed{}$ $\quad$ $5 + 7 + 3 = \boxed{}$

5. $2 + 9 + 6 = \boxed{}$ $\quad$ $6 + 1 + 9 = \boxed{}$ $\quad$ $7 + 7 + 4 = \boxed{}$

6. $1 + 8 + 3 = \boxed{}$ $\quad$ $6 + 6 + 3 = \boxed{}$ $\quad$ $2 + 7 + 3 = \boxed{}$

7. **On the Back** Explain why it doesn't matter which order you use to add three numbers.

Add Three Numbers

Name _____

Class Activity

Vocabulary
centimeter
length
line segment

▶ **Count Centimeter Lengths**

A **centimeter** is a unit of measure for **length**. The short way to write centimeters is cm.

⊢——⊣
1 cm

You can make a 6-cm **line segment** by pushing together six 1-cm line lengths.

— —— —— —— —— ——
————————————————

You can mark the 1-cm lengths.

⊢—+—+—+—+—+—⊣

To find the measure of the line segment, count the 1-cm lengths.

Use a centimeter ruler to mark the 1-cm lengths.
Count the 1-cm lengths.

1. _____ ☐ cm

2. _____ ☐ cm

3. _____ ☐ cm

Class Activity

Name _____

Vocabulary

line segment
horizontal
vertical

▶ **Draw Line Segments**

You can use a ruler to draw a **line segment** 7 cm long.
Begin drawing at the zero edge of your ruler. Stop
when you have counted seven 1-cm lengths.

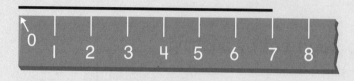

Use your centimeter ruler to draw a **horizontal** line
segment with the length given. Mark off and count
1-cm lengths to check the length.

4. 8 cm

5. 5 cm

6. Draw a **vertical** line segment 3 cm long.
Mark off and count 1-cm lengths to check the length.

Rulers, Lengths, and Partner Lengths

▶**The Ruler as a Group of Lengths**

> You can think of a ruler as a group of line segments
> with different lengths.

7. Copy this group of line segments.

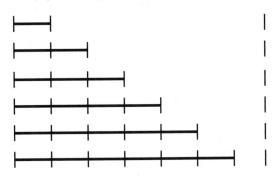

8. Next, draw the same group of line segments
   closer together.

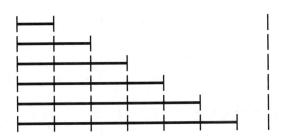

9. Write the number of centimeters at the end of
   each line segment.

10. Imagine that you drew the segments so close
    together that they were on top of each other.
    What would the segments start to look like?

_____

11. Place a centimeter ruler under your diagram.
    What do the numbers on the ruler mean?

_____

Name _____

Class Activity

Vocabulary

partner lengths

▶ **Explore Partner Lengths**

12. Show the **partner lengths** for a 6-cm line segment.

Partners	**Partner Lengths**	**Equations**

☐ and ☐ ——————————— $6 =$ ☐ $+$ ☐

☐ and ☐ ——————————— $6 =$ ☐ $+$ ☐

☐ and ☐ ——————————— $6 =$ ☐ $+$ ☐

13. How many pairs of partner lengths does the 6-cm line segment have?

_____ pairs

Rulers, Lengths, and Partner Lengths

Dear Family,

Your child is working on a geometry unit. In this unit, children will use centimeter rulers to measure lines, draw shapes, and find perimeters of shapes.

You can help your child link geometry concepts learned in school with the real world. Encourage your child to find examples of rectangles, squares, and triangles in your home or neighborhood. This will help your child enjoy and understand geometry.

Look for shapes in

- books
- road signs
- food packaging

- newspaper pages
- window panes
- the front of your home

In Lesson 1 of this unit, your child will be asked to find the partner lengths of a line segment for homework. An example is shown below.

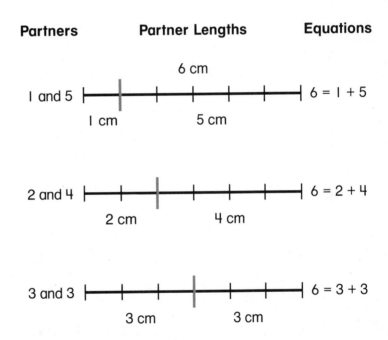

If you have any questions or comments, please call or write to me. Thank you.

Sincerely,
Your child's teacher.

Estimada familia:

Su niño está trabajando en una unidad sobre geometría. En esta unidad los estudiantes usarán reglas en centímetros para medir rectas, trazar figuras y hallar perímetros de figuras.

Puede ayudar a su niño a relacionar los conceptos de geometría que aprende en la escuela con el mundo real. Anime a su niño a buscar ejemplos de rectángulos, cuadrados y triángulos en su casa o en el vecindario. Esto ayudará a su niño a disfrutar de la geometría y a comprenderla.

Busquen figuras en:

- libros
- señales viales
- envases de alimentos

- páginas de periódicos
- vidrios de ventanas
- la fachada de su casa

En la Lección 1 de esta unidad se le pedirá a su niño que halle las "longitudes compañeras" de un segmento de recta como parte de la tarea. Abajo se muestra un ejemplo.

Compañeros   **Longitudes compañeras**   **Ecuaciones**

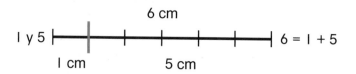

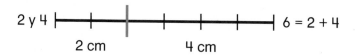

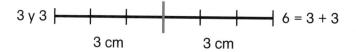

Si tiene alguna pregunta o comentario, por favor comuníquese conmigo. Gracias.

Atentamente,
El maestro de su niño

Rulers, Lengths, and Partner Lengths

Vocabulary

square

▶ **Draw and Identify Squares**

A **square** is a shape with four equal sides and four square corners.

1. Use your centimeter ruler. Draw a square with sides that are each 3 cm long.

Look at these shapes.

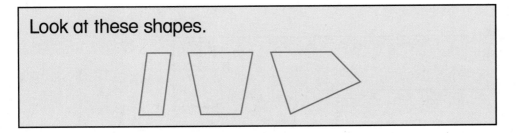

2. Are any of these shapes squares? _____

3. How are the corners of these shapes different from the corners of squares?

_____

4. How are the sides of these shapes different from the sides of squares?

_____

5. Is this shape a square? Explain why or why not.

_____

_____

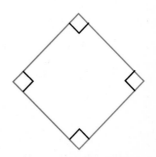

Class Activity

Name _____

Vocabulary

rectangle

▶ Draw and Identify Rectangles

> A **rectangle** is a shape with opposite sides that are equal in length and four square corners.

6. Use your centimeter ruler to draw a rectangle that is 6 cm long and 3 cm wide.

> Look at these shapes.

7. Are these shapes rectangles? Explain why or why not.

_____

_____

8. Is a square a rectangle? Explain why or why not.

_____

_____

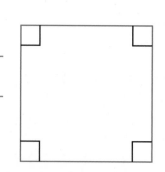

Squares, Rectangles, and Triangles

Vocabulary

triangle

▶ **Compare Lengths of Sides of Triangles**

A **triangle** is a shape with three corners and three straight sides. All of these shapes are triangles.

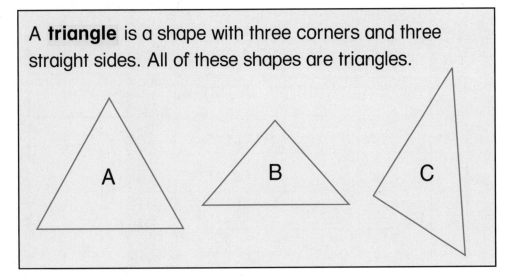

9. Measure each side of triangle A. What did you discover about the sides?

_____

_____

10. Measure each side of triangle B. What did you discover about the sides?

_____

_____

11. Measure each side of triangle C. What did you discover about the sides?

_____

_____

12. **On the Back** Draw a triangle using your centimeter ruler.
    • It must have a square corner.
    • It must have a horizontal side that is 12 cm long.
    • It must have a vertical side that is 16 cm long.

Squares, Rectangles, and Triangles

Vocabulary
perimeter
square

▶ ## Perimeters of Squares

> **Perimeter** is the distance around the outside of a shape.

Find the perimeter of each **square**.

1.

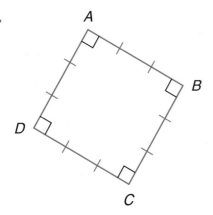

$P =$ ☐ cm

2.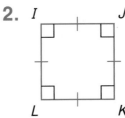

$P =$ ☐ cm

Use a centimeter ruler. Find the perimeter of each square.

3.

Z ◇ X
W
Y

$P =$ ☐ cm

4.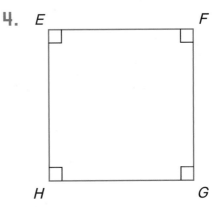

$P =$ ☐ cm

► **Perimeters of Rectangles**

Perimeter is the distance around the outside of a shape.

Find the perimeter of each **rectangle**.

5.

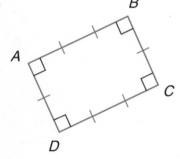

$P = \boxed{}$ cm

6.

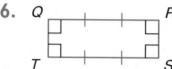

$P = \boxed{}$ cm

Use a centimeter ruler. Find the perimeter of each rectangle.

7.

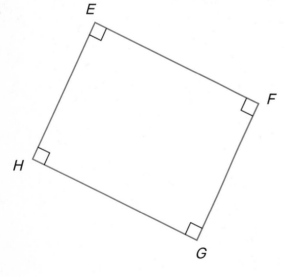

$P = \boxed{}$ cm

8.

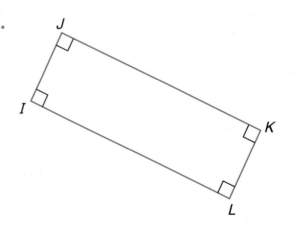

$P = \boxed{}$ cm

Perimeters of Squares and Rectangles

Class Activity

▶ **Perimeters of Triangles**

Find the **perimeter** of each **triangle**.

1.

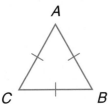

2.

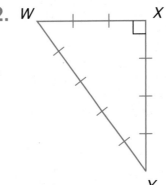

$P = \boxed{}$ cm

$P = \boxed{}$ cm

Use a centimeter ruler. Find the perimeter of each triangle.

3.

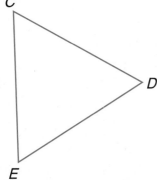

4.

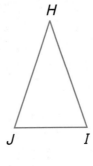

$P = \boxed{}$ cm

$P = \boxed{}$ cm

5. **On the Back** Use a centimeter ruler. Draw a triangle. Measure each side. **Round** the measures if you need to. Find the perimeter.

Perimeters of Triangles

1. Measure the line segment. Mark and count 1-cm lengths.

———————————————————   ☐ cm

2. Draw a line segment 6 cm long.

3. Draw line segments 7 cm long to show all the partner lengths. Write the partners and the equations for each.

Partners	**Partner Lengths**	**Equations**
☐ and ☐		7 = ☐ + ☐
☐ and ☐		7 = ☐ + ☐
☐ and ☐		7 = ☐ + ☐

4. Draw a square with a side 3 cm long.

5. Draw any triangle with one side 4 cm long and another side 5 cm long.

6. Draw a rectangle that is 6 cm long and 2 cm wide.

Use a centimeter ruler. Find the perimeter of each shape.

7.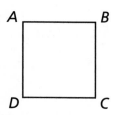

Perimeter = ☐ cm

8.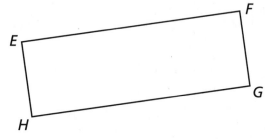

Perimeter = ☐ cm

9.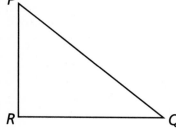

Perimeter = ☐ cm

10. Extended Response How are squares and rectangles the same? How are they different?

_____

_____

_____

_____

Class Activity

Name _____

Vocabulary
change plus
change minus

▶ **Solve and Discuss**

Solve the story problems.

Show your work.

1. Last year our school had 5 computers in the library. They bought some more over the summer. Now there are 12. How many computers did they buy over the summer?

computer

☐ _____
　　　label

2. Alina had 17 beads. She used 9 of them to make a bracelet. How many beads does she have left?

beads

☐ _____
　　　label

3. Erin wrapped 6 party favors. She needs to wrap 15 favors in all. How many favors does she still need to wrap?

party favors

☐ _____
　　　label

 4. **On the Back** Write and solve your own **change plus** story problem or **change minus** story problem. Show a Proof Drawing.

Name _____

_____

_____

_____

_____

_____

_____

_____

_____

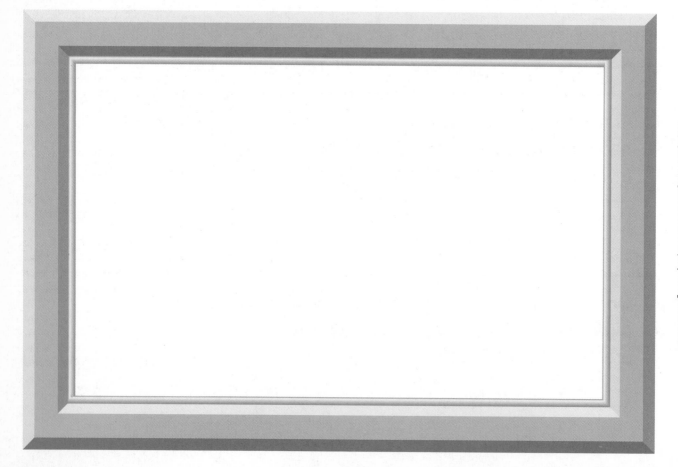

Change Plus and Change Minus Story Problems

Dear Family,

Your child is learning to solve story problems called *change plus* and *change minus* problems. These problems begin with a given quantity that is then modified by change—something is added or subtracted—which results in a new quantity.

Proof Drawings show what your child was thinking when solving the problem. It is important that children label their drawings to link them to the problem situation.

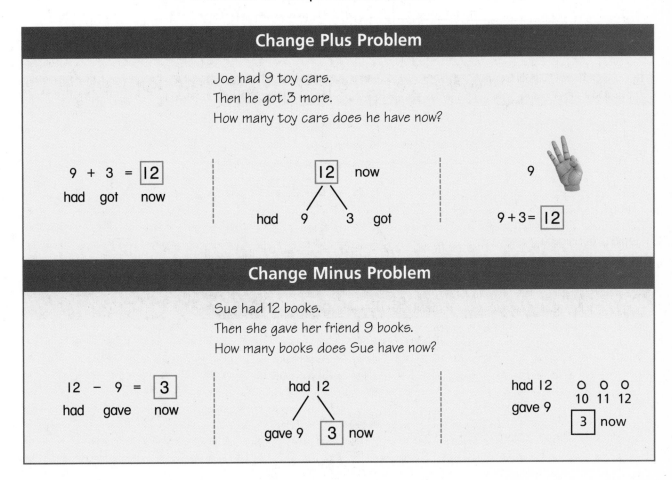

Change Plus Problem

Joe had 9 toy cars.
Then he got 3 more.
How many toy cars does he have now?

9 + 3 = 12
had   got   now

12 now
had 9   3 got

9
9 + 3 = 12

Change Minus Problem

Sue had 12 books.
Then she gave her friend 9 books.
How many books does Sue have now?

12 − 9 = 3
had   gave   now

had 12
gave 9   3 now

had 12
gave 9   O O O
           10 11 12
           3 now

Please call if you have any questions or concerns. Thank you for helping your child learn about change plus and change minus problems.

Sincerely,
Your child's teacher

Estimada familia:

Su niño está aprendiendo a resolver problemas en los que se modifica una cantidad al sumar o al restar. Éstos empiezan con una cantidad dada que luego es modificada por un cambio (algo que se suma o se resta), lo que resulta en una nueva cantidad.

Los dibujos muestran lo que su niño estaba pensando mientras resolvía el problema. Es importante que los niños rotulen sus dibujos para relacionarlos con la situación del problema.

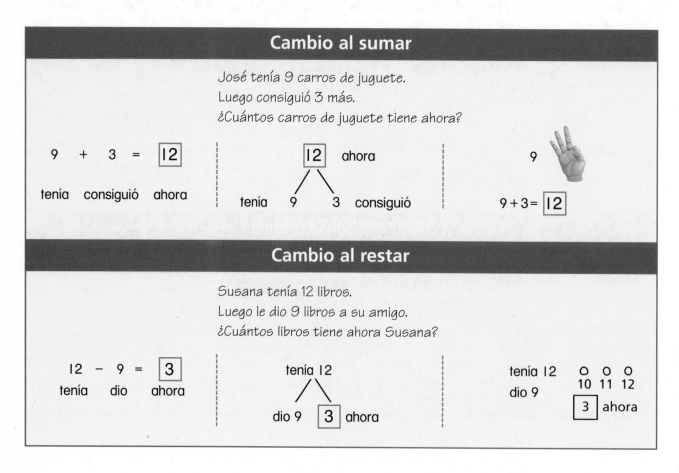

Cambio al sumar

José tenía 9 carros de juguete.
Luego consiguió 3 más.
¿Cuántos carros de juguete tiene ahora?

9 + 3 = 12

tenía consiguió ahora

12 ahora

tenía 9 3 consiguió

9

9 + 3 = 12

Cambio al restar

Susana tenía 12 libros.
Luego le dio 9 libros a su amigo.
¿Cuántos libros tiene ahora Susana?

12 − 9 = 3
tenía dio ahora

tenía 12

dio 9 3 ahora

tenía 12
dio 9

O O O
10 11 12

3 ahora

Si tiene alguna pregunta o comentario, por favor comuníquese conmigo. Gracias por ayudar a su niño a aprender problemas con combios al sumar o al restar.

Atentamente,
El maestro de su niño

Change Plus and Change Minus Story Problems

Class Activity

Name _____

▶ **Solve and Discuss**

Make a Proof Drawing to solve the story problems.

Show your work.

1. Brian had some tomato plants in his garden. 9 of the plants were eaten by bugs. 4 plants are left. How many plants did Brian have in the beginning?

   [ ] _____
       label

   bug

2. Heather bought 5 puzzles at a yard sale. Then her brother gave her some more. Now she has a total of 11 puzzles. How many puzzles did her brother give her?

   [ ] _____
       label

   puzzle

3. I had 16 pounds of potatoes. I used some to make potato salad. Now I have 7 pounds of potatoes left. How many pounds did I use?

   [ ] _____
       label

   potatoes

➡ 4. **On the Back** Create your own **change plus** story problem or **change minus** story problem about books. Make a Proof Drawing.

Name

More Change Plus and Change Minus Story Problems

Class Activity

▶ **Solve and Discuss**

Draw a Proof Drawing to solve the story problems.

Show your work.

1. There are 13 people in a bike race. 8 are on top of the hill. The rest are at the bottom of the hill. How many people are at the bottom of the hill?

   ☐ _____
          label

hill

2. 4 horses are in the barn. 8 horses are in the field. How many horses are on the farm altogether?

   ☐ _____
          label

horse

3. Andrew made some sandwiches. 6 are turkey sandwiches and 7 are ham sandwiches. How many sandwiches did Andrew make in all?

   ☐ _____
          label

sandwich

4. **On the Back** Write a **collection story problem** using the numbers 5 and 8. Then draw a Proof Drawing to show how to solve it.

Name _____

_____

_____

_____

_____

_____

_____

_____

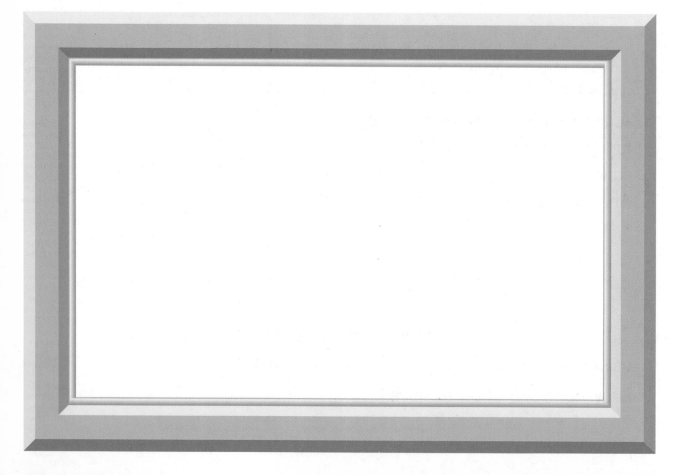

Collection Problems

Vocabulary

Venn diagram

▶ **Introduce Venn Diagrams**

Fill in the **Venn diagrams** to show some
things that belong together.

I.

Flowers

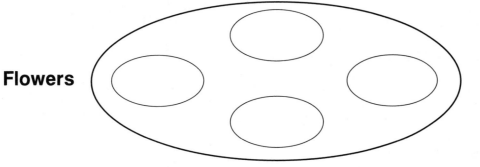

2.

Pets

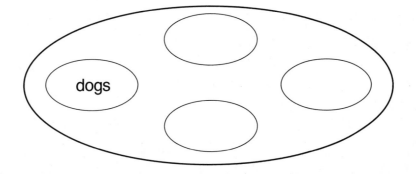

3. **Create and Explain** Create your own **Venn diagram**
and explain the steps you took.

_____
Group Name

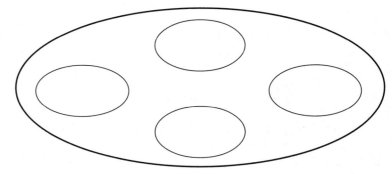

_____

_____

_____

Class Activity

▶ **Solve and Discuss**

Make a Proof Drawing to solve the
story problems.

Show your work.

4. I have 12 flowers in a vase. 8 are daisies.
   The rest are roses. How many are roses?

   ☐ _____
        label

rose

5. There are 13 animals at the shelter.
   7 of them are dogs. The rest are cats.
   How many cats are at the shelter?

   ☐ _____
        label

animal
shelter

6. Walt saw 4 crows. Then he saw some
   finches at the feeder. He saw 12 birds in
   all. How many finches were there?

   ☐ _____
        label

finch

▶ **You Decide**

Complete this problem.

7. Jenna has 4 _____ and
   Bill has 6 _____ . How
   many _____ do they
   have altogether?

   ☐ _____
        label

Story Problems with Group Names

Dear Family,

Your child is now learning to solve story problems. Some of these problems are a special kind of "no-action" problem. The people or objects in these problems may be grouped together into a larger category to solve the problem. For example, 5 oranges and 4 apples are 9 pieces of fruit; 3 boys and 7 girls are 10 children. Having children group and then classify everyday objects is helpful for both math and language development.

One way to illustrate categories is to use a Venn diagram. A Venn diagram is a drawing that uses overlapping shapes to show how things are related. In the completed example shown below, each thing (maple, oak, pine, and elm) fits into the larger category: trees.

Children may work from the larger category to the smaller (Name some trees.), or from the smaller category to the larger (How are maple, oak, pine, and elm alike? They are all kinds of trees.) You might want to play a game with your child, taking turns creating Venn diagrams and guessing the category or adding examples to a given category. You may have more or fewer than four examples inside the larger category.

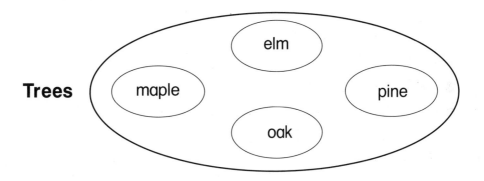

Please call if you have any questions or comments.

Sincerely,
Your child's teacher

Estimada familia:

Su niño está aprendiendo a resolver problemas verbales. Algunos de ellos pertenecen a un tipo especial de problemas que no contienen acción. Para resolver el problema, las personas u objetos que aparecen en él se pueden agrupar en una categoría más grande. Por ejemplo, 5 naranjas y 4 manzanas son 9 frutas; 3 niños y 7 niñas son 10 niños. Pedirles a los niños que agrupen y luego clasifiquen objetos de uso diario es útil para el desarrollo matemático y del lenguaje.

Una manera de ilustrar categorías es usar un diagrama de Venn. Un diagrama de Venn es un dibujo que utiliza figuras superpuestas para mostrar cómo se relacionan las cosas. En el ejemplo terminado que se muestra abajo, cada cosa (arce, roble, pino y olmo) pertenece a la categoría más grande: árboles.

Los niños pueden trabajar de la categoría más grande a la más pequeña (Nombren algunos árboles.), o de la categoría más pequeña a la más grande (¿En qué se parecen el arce, el roble, el pino y el olmo? Todos son un tipo de árbol.). Usted puede jugar con su niño turnándose para crear diagramas de Venn y adivinar la categoría, o agregando ejemplos a una categoría dada. Dentro de la categoría más grande puede incluir más o menos de cuatro ejemplos.

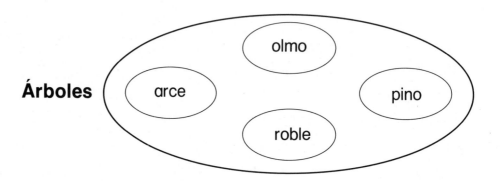

Si tiene alguna pregunta o comentario, por favor comuníquese conmigo.

Atentamente,
El maestro de su niño

Story Problems with Group Names

Class Activity

Name

comparison story problems
more   fewer
most   fewest

▶ **Solve and Discuss**

Draw a picture to solve the
comparison story problems.

Show your work.

1. Barbara has 11 videos to return to the
   movie store. If Barbara returns 4 videos,
   she will have as many videos as Dale. How
   many videos does Dale have?

   video

   ☐ _____
           label

2. Shelley washed 14 cars. Amir washed 9
   cars. How many **more** cars did Shelley
   wash than Amir?

   car

   ☐ _____
           label

3. Gale has 6 grapes in a basket. Carl has
   grapes too. If Gale gets 5 more grapes, he
   will have as many grapes as Carl. How
   many grapes does Carl have?

   basket

   ☐ _____
           label

4. **On the Back** Meg has 10 stamps. Greg has
   5 **fewer** stamps than Meg. Sora has 2 more stamps
   than Greg. Who has the **most** stamps? Who has the
   fewest stamps? Explain.

Name

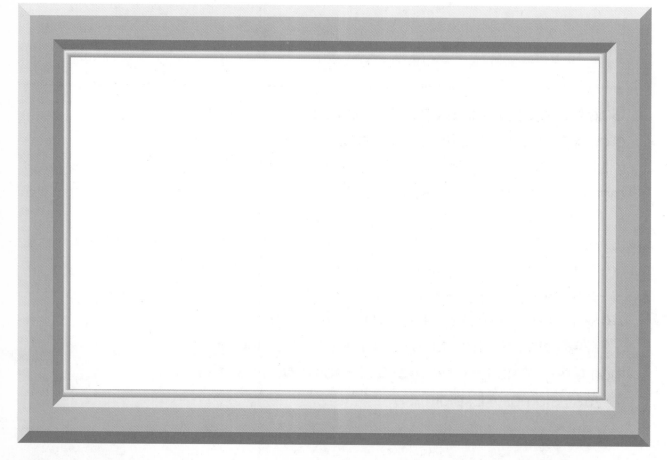

Comparison Story Problems

Class Activity

Name

▶ **Solve and Discuss**

Solve the comparison story problems.

Show your work.

---

1. Haley has 13 books in her bag. Gabrielle has 8 books in her bag. How many **fewer** books does Gabrielle have in her bag than Haley?

bag

□ _____
  label

---

2. Hannah has 11 stickers. Nat has 3 stickers. How many fewer stickers does Nat have than Hannah?

sticker

□ _____
  label

---

3. An eraser costs 7 cents. A pencil costs 9 cents **more** than an eraser. How many cents does a pencil cost?

pencil

□ _____
  label

---

4. My friend has 7 cherries. If I eat 4 cherries, I will have as many cherries as my friend. How many cherries do I have?

cherries

□ _____
  label

Going Further

► **Use Logical Thinking**

Solve the story problems.

Show your work.

1. Ty has 3 more red cars than blue cars. He has 2 fewer blue cars than green cars. He has 6 green cars. How many red cars does he have? How many blue cars does he have?

red cars _____ blue cars _____

2. The ball costs less than the truck. The truck costs less than the plane. The plane costs the most. What is the cost of each toy?

$5.00

$2.00

$6.00

ball _____ truck _____ plane _____

3. Craig and Orna each bought one of the books shown. Craig spent $2 more than Orna. Which book did each child buy?

Cats $6   Birds $5   Dogs $7

Craig _____ Orna _____

4. **Critical Thinking** Solve the story problem. Ellen, Jay, and Ali are measuring how tall they are. Jay is shorter than Ali. Ali is the tallest. Ellen is taller than Jay. List the children in order from shortest to tallest.

_____   _____   _____

shortest   tallest

More Comparison Story Problems

Parachute Drop
Teen Totals

$8 + 7 = \boxed{15}$ $7 + \boxed{6} = 13$ $17 - 8 = \boxed{9}$

$8 + 8 = \boxed{16}$ $3 + \boxed{9} = 12$ $14 - 8 = \boxed{6}$

$9 + 4 = \boxed{13}$ $5 + \boxed{6} = 11$ $17 - 9 = \boxed{8}$

$6 + 9 = \boxed{15}$ $5 + \boxed{7} = 12$ $18 - 9 = \boxed{9}$

$2 + 9 = \boxed{11}$ $9 + \boxed{6} = 15$ $12 - 8 = \boxed{4}$

$6 + 8 = \boxed{14}$ $5 + \boxed{9} = 14$ $15 - 7 = \boxed{8}$

$6 + 5 = \boxed{11}$ $7 + \boxed{5} = 12$ $12 - 6 = \boxed{6}$

$3 + 8 = \boxed{11}$ $7 + \boxed{9} = 16$ $13 - 6 = \boxed{7}$

$9 + 5 = \boxed{14}$ $9 + \boxed{3} = 12$ $11 - 9 = \boxed{2}$

$8 + 5 = \boxed{13}$ $7 + \boxed{7} = 14$ $11 - 4 = \boxed{7}$

$7 + 6 = \boxed{13}$ $8 + \boxed{3} = 11$ $16 - 9 = \boxed{7}$

Mixed Story Problems

Class Activity

Name _____

▶ **Solve and Discuss**

Solve the story problems.   Show your work.

---

1. Erica has 13 colored pencils. She has
   8 at home and some at school. How
   many are at school?

   ☐ _____
     label

pencil

---

2. Joan has 15 toy guitars. Delia has
   7 toy guitars. How many fewer toy guitars
   does Delia have than Joan?

   ☐ _____
     label

guitar

---

3. Alvin had 14 puppets. He gave some
   to his brother. Now Alvin has 5
   puppets left. How many puppets did
   Alvin give to his brother?

   ☐ _____
     label

puppet

---

4. Yolanda has a box of tennis balls. Eddie
   took 7 of them. Now Yolanda has 5 left.
   How many tennis balls did Yolanda have
   in the beginning?

   ☐ _____
     label

tennis ball

Going Further

▶ **Find Information in a Table**

The table shows how the second graders at Smith Elementary get to school. Use the table to solve the problems.

Ways to Get to School

Way	Number of Children
Bus	15
Car	7
Bike	9
Walk	14

1. How many children ride a bus to school?

   _____

Show your work.

2. How many children ride a bike to school?

   _____

3. How many more children ride a bus to school than ride a bike?

   _____

4. How many fewer children ride a bike than walk to school?

   _____

5. How many children either ride a bike or ride in a car to get to school?

   _____

▶ **Number Sense**

Use the table to complete the sentences.

6. Almost the same number of children ride a bus as

   _____ .

7. Almost the same number of children ride a bike as

   _____ .

8. More children ride a bike than _____ .

Mixed Story Problems

Class Activity

Name

► Complete and Solve Story Problems

Add information so you can solve the problems. Then solve the story problems.

Show your work.

1. Shannon made a pitcher of lemonade. She used 8 lemons. How many lemons did she have left?

pitcher

_____

[ ] _____
       label

2. Sam walked his dog in the morning and again in the afternoon. Altogether Sam and the dog walked 15 blocks. How far did they walk in the morning?

dog

_____

[ ] _____
       label

3. Kamille made a bracelet with blue and purple beads. 6 beads are blue. How many beads are purple?

beads

_____

[ ] _____
       label

Class Activity

Name _____

▶ **Solve Problems with Extra Information**

Cross out the extra information. Solve.

Show your work.

---

1. The dentist had 8 red toothbrushes and 6 green ones. Then she bought 9 more red ones. How many red toothbrushes does she have now?

   ☐ _____
          label

toothbrush

---

2. Jory walked 9 miles around the lake. Then he walked 4 miles around the pond. He usually bicycles 18 miles a day. How many miles did he walk today?

   ☐ _____
          label

pond

---

3. Pam had 7 long ribbons and 9 short ribbons. She gave away 5 short ones. How many short ribbons does Pam have now?

   ☐ _____
          label

ribbon

---

4. On Friday, Mr. Lopez rescued 5 animals. On Saturday, he rescued 8 animals. He drove 7 miles. How many animals did he rescue in all?

   ☐ _____
          label

animals

Problems with Not Enough or Extra Information

Going Further

Name _____

▶ **Find Information in a Story**

The Zoo
Today my class went to the zoo. I saw 4 elephants and 5 tigers. The giraffes were tall. There were 8 monkeys playing. I counted 13 penguins. I had fun at the zoo.
By Robbie

Use the story to solve the problems.

Show your work.

1. How many more monkeys than tigers did Robbie see?

   ☐ _____
      label

monkey

2. How many more penguins than elephants did Robbie see?

   ☐ _____
      label

elephant

3. How many fewer tigers than penguins did Robbie see?

   ☐ _____
      label

penguin

4. **On the Back** Write and solve another problem about Robbie's day at the zoo.

Problems with Not Enough or Extra Information

▶ Practice Solving Story Problems

Cross out extra information. Write missing or
hidden information. Solve the problems.

Show your work.

1. Chris washed some cars at the car wash. His
   friend Kelly washed some cars at the car wash.
   They washed a total of 16 cars. How many cars
   did Kelly wash?

car wash

☐ _____
      label

2. Shanna put 13 markers and 6 crayons in her
   book bag. When she got to school, she gave 4
   of the markers to her friend. How many markers
   does Shanna have left?

marker

☐ _____
      label

3. There are 9 children and a set of triplets in the
   library. How many children are in the library?

library

☐ _____
      label

Going Further

▶ **Research Information**

Use the numbers below for exercises 1–7.

3	7	12	24	31	60	100

1. Number of days in a week _____

2. Number of months in a year _____

3. Number of seconds in a minute _____

4. Number of hours in a day _____

5. Number of feet in a yard _____

6. Number of days in July _____

7. Number of yards on a football field _____

Solve the problem.

8. Suzanne was on vacation for two weeks. How many days was Suzanne on vacation?

☐ _____
   label

Problems with Hidden Information and Mixed Practice

Class Activity

▶ **Solve Two-Step Story Problems**

Solve the **two-step story problems**.

Show your work.

1. Lana had 9 sheep and some horses on her farm. Altogether there were 17 animals. Her grandmother gave her 2 more horses. How many horses does she have now?

sheep

☐ _____
    label

2. There are 14 computers in the school library. 5 girls and 3 boys are using the computers right now. How many more students can use a computer?

library

☐ _____
    label

3. There were 15 packages at the post office. 6 were sent out. Then, people brought in 8 more. How many packages are at the post office now?

package

☐ _____
    label

4. Mrs. Yu has 4 yellow flowers, 5 white flowers, and some purple flowers in a vase. She has a total of 18 flowers. How many purple flowers are in the vase?

vase

☐ _____
    label

Going Further

► **Choose a Reasonable Answer**

Ring the most reasonable answer.

1. There are 9 boys in the spelling bee. There are fewer girls than boys in the spelling bee. How many girls could be in the spelling bee?

   6 girls   10 girls   20 girls

2. Rosa has some pennies, 5 nickels, and 4 dimes. She has a total of 17 coins. How many pennies does Rosa have?

   1 penny   8 pennies   18 pennies

3. Kim has to read 14 pages in her book. She reads 5 pages. How many pages does she have left to read?

   19 pages   14 pages   9 pages

4. Willie collected 9 shells. He gave 4 shells to his sister. Then he found 6 more shells. How many shells does Willie have now?

   5 shells   11 shells   19 shells

5. Cara and Jason collect baseball cards. Jason has 38 cards. Cara has a few more cards than Jason. About how many cards could she have?

   20 cards   41 cards   80 cards

Two-Step Story Problems

Name _____

Class Activity

▶ **Two-Step Story Problems**

Solve the two-step story problems.

Show your work.

1. Aretha has 7 whistles. She has 4 more whistles than Jeremy. How many whistles do Aretha and Jeremy have altogether?

☐ _____
   label

whistle

2. Mina buys 4 shirts and 5 skirts. She returns 2 skirts to the store. How many new pieces of clothing does Mina keep?

☐ _____
   label

clothing

3. Ed bought 9 bananas at one fruit stand and 3 at another. He bought 8 more bananas than Gail. How many did Gail buy?

☐ _____
   label

fruit stand

4. Felix had 7 pounds of white potatoes and 8 pounds of red potatoes to cook for the celebration. First he cooked 6 pounds. How many pounds of potatoes does he still have to cook?

☐ _____
   label

potatoes

Extra Practice

Name _____

▶ **Add Using Doubles Plus 1 and
Doubles Minus 1 Strategies**

1. Add.

A. $4 + 5 =$ ☐	**E.** $3 + 2 =$ ☐	**O.** $8 + 9 =$ ☐
T. $7 + 6 =$ ☐	**L.** $4 + 3 =$ ☐	**W.** $7 + 8 =$ ☐
E. $2 + 3 =$ ☐	**T.** $6 + 7 =$ ☐	**W.** $8 + 7 =$ ☐
S. $\begin{array}{r} 3 \\ + 4 \\ \hline \end{array}$	**T.** $\begin{array}{r} 6 \\ + 7 \\ \hline \end{array}$	**L.** $\begin{array}{r} 5 \\ + 6 \\ \hline \end{array}$
O. $\begin{array}{r} 9 \\ + 8 \\ \hline \end{array}$	**A.** $\begin{array}{r} 5 \\ + 4 \\ \hline \end{array}$	**L.** $\begin{array}{r} 6 \\ + 5 \\ \hline \end{array}$

2. Use the letters for each answer to help you solve the riddle.

What gets wetter the more it dries?

Answer:

___ ___ ___ ___ ___ ___
 9   13   17   15   5   11

Strategies Using Doubles

Class Activity

Name _____

▶ **Story Problems**

Solve the story problems.

Show your work.

---

1. Our school has 12 computers. 7 are in the computer room. The rest are in the library. How many are in the library?

   [ ] _____
   label

computer

---

2. When I got my puppy, he weighed 9 pounds. He gained 7 pounds since then. His mother weighs 32 pounds. How much does my puppy weigh now?

   [ ] _____
   label

puppy

---

3. 14 strings on Jenna's harp were out of tune. Then she tuned some of them. She has 8 more to tune. How many strings did she already tune?

   [ ] _____
   label

harp

---

4. The zoo has 5 bears, 4 hippos, and some leopards. If the total number of bears, hippos, and leopards at the zoo is 18, how many leopards are there?

   [ ] _____
   label

leopard

Name _____

Extra Practice

▶ **Mixed Story Problems**

Solve the story problems.

Show your work.

1. There were 7 bicycles in the rack. 5 were red and 2 were blue. Then 6 more children put their bicycles in the rack. How many bicycles are in the rack now?

bicycle

☐ _____
    label

2. Corey has 6 books in his bag. He has 6 more books in his bag than Angela has in her bag. How many books are there in the two bags altogether?

book

☐ _____
    label

3. The ice cube tray holds 14 ice cubes. Kacey and Riley put some ice cubes in their glasses. Kacey put 5 cubes in her glass. 3 cubes were left in the tray. How many cubes did Riley put in his glass?

ice cube

☐ _____
    label

4. The cook is making a dozen toasted cheese sandwiches. He has made 7. How many more does he have to make?

cheese

☐ _____
    label

Mixed Practice and Writing Story Problems

Solve each story problem.

Show your work.

---

1. Jenna has 11 goldfish. She gives some
   to her friend. Now she has only 7 goldfish.
   How many goldfish did she give to
   her friend?

   [ ] _____
        label

goldfish

---

2. There are 8 puzzle pieces on the table.
   Kay put 4 more on the table. How many
   puzzle pieces are on the table now?

   [ ] _____
        label

table

---

3. Joey had a bag of peanuts. He gave
   8 peanuts to his friends. Then he had
   7 left. How many peanuts were in
   the bag?

   [ ] _____
        label

peanuts

Solve each story problem.

Show your work.

4. There are 12 apples in a bowl. 5 of them are red. The rest are green. How many apples are green?

bowl

☐ _____
   label

5. Makala buys 9 plums from the fruit stand. Trin buys plums, too. If Makala buys 7 more plums, she will have as many plums as Trin. How many plums does Trin have?

plum

☐ _____
   label

6. Darnel and Amelia have baseball caps for sale. Darnel sells 14 baseball caps. Amelia sells 9 baseball caps. How many fewer caps does Amelia sell than Darnel?

baseball cap

☐ _____
   label

Name _____

Solve each story problem.
Cross out any extra information.

Show your work.

7. Franny has 8 kittens and 2 dogs. 4 kittens
   are asleep. How many kittens are awake?

   ☐ _____
        label

   kitten

8. Evan read a book each day for a week.
   The next day he read 3 books. How many
   books did Evan read altogether?

   ☐ _____
        label

   book

9. There are 6 seals, a walrus, and some
   dolphins in the water. There are a total of
   15 animals in the water. How many
   dolphins are in the water?

   ☐ _____
        label

   walrus

10. **Extended Response** Write and solve a subtraction story problem using the numbers 9 and 6.

_____

_____

_____

_____

_____

Answer: ☐ _____
        label

Test

▶ **Observations about Shapes and Perimeter**

What I Know about Squares

What I Know about Rectangles

What I Know about Triangles

Name _____

Share Observations about Geometry

Dear Family,

Your child is beginning a new unit in geometry. In this unit, children will be learning about shapes that have four sides. Shapes with four sides are called *quadrilaterals.*

These are examples of quadrilaterals:

square   rectangle   parallelogram   quadrilateral

square: It has four square corners and four sides of equal length.

rectangle: It has four square corners and opposite sides of equal length.

parallelogram: It has two pairs of parallel sides.

quadrilateral: It has four sides.

Some shapes can be described by more than one of these terms.

In this unit, your child will learn to identify all of the terms that can be used to describe a quadrilateral. For example, your child will be asked to mark each term that identifies a particular shape.

☑ quadrilateral   ☑ quadrilateral   ☑ quadrilateral   ☑ quadrilateral
☑ parallelogram   ☑ parallelogram   ☑ parallelogram   ☐ parallelogram
☑ rectangle   ☑ rectangle   ☐ rectangle   ☐ rectangle
☑ square   ☐ square   ☐ square   ☐ square

If you have any questions or comments, please call or write to me. Thank you.

Sincerely,
Your child's teacher

Estimada familia:

Su niño está comenzando una nueva unidad de geometría. En esta unidad, los niños aprenderán acerca de figuras que tienen cuatro lados. Las figuras de cuatro lados se llaman *cuadriláteros*.

Éstos son ejemplos de cuadriláteros:

cuadrado rectángulo paralelogramo cuadrilátero

cuadrado: tiene cuatro vértices rectos y cuatro lados de igual longitud.

rectángulo: tiene cuatro vértices rectos y lados opuestos de igual longitud.

paralelogramo: tiene dos pares de lados paralelos.

cuadrilátero: tiene cuatro lados.

Algunas figuras se pueden describir con más de uno de estos términos.

En esta unidad, su niño aprenderá a identificar todos los términos usados para describir un cuadrilátero. Por ejemplo, se le pedirá a su niño que marque cada término que identifique una figura en particular.

☑ cuadrilátero	☑ cuadrilátero	☑ cuadrilátero	☑ cuadrilátero
☑ paralelogramo	☑ paralelogramo	☑ paralelogramo	☐ paralelogramo
☑ rectángulo	☑ rectángulo	☐ rectángulo	☐ rectángulo
☑ cuadrado	☐ cuadrado	☐ cuadrado	☐ cuadrado

Si tiene alguna pregunta o comentario, por favor comuníquese conmigo. Gracias.

Atentamente,
El maestro de su niño

Share Observations about Geometry

Class Activity

Vocabulary

parallel
parallelogram

▶ **Parallel Lines**

Parallel lines never cross.

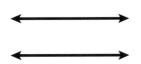

▶ **Parallelograms**

Parallelograms have four sides, and opposite sides are parallel.

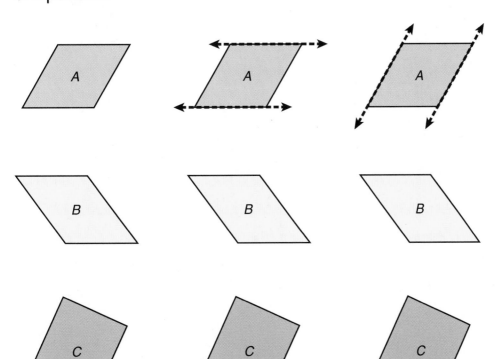

Class Activity

▶ **Draw Parallelograms**

In each row draw three more parallelograms.
The first row is done for you.

1.

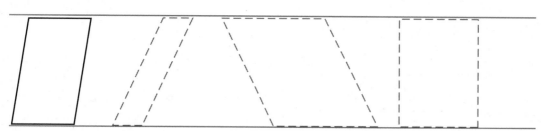

2.

3.

4.

5.

Define Parallel Lines and Parallelograms

Going Further

▶ **Hidden Parallelograms**

Find the hidden parallelograms.
Two are done for you.

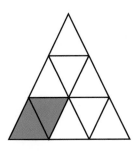 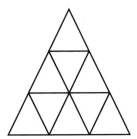 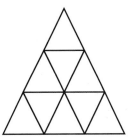 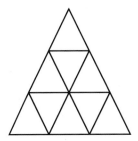

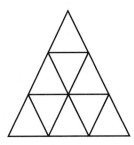 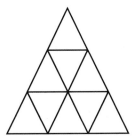 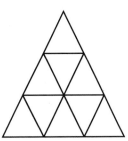 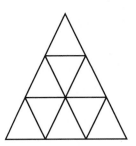

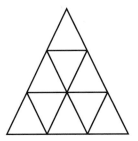 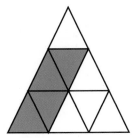 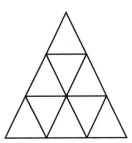 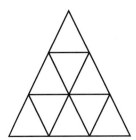

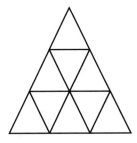 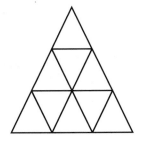 

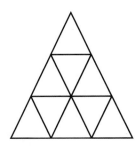

Define Parallel Lines and Parallelograms

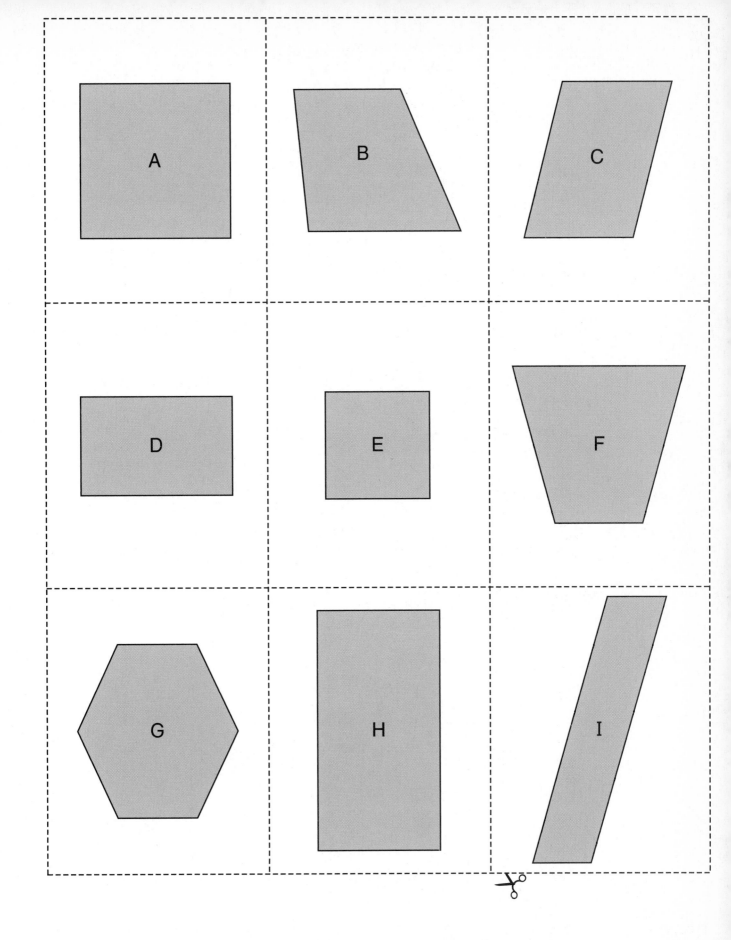

Relate Different Quadrilaterals **131**

Relate Different Quadrilaterals

▶ **Name Quadrilaterals**

Place a check mark beside each word that names the shape.

1.

[shape: rectangle]

☐ quadrilateral

☐ parallelogram

☐ rectangle

☐ square

2.

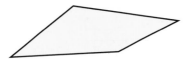

☐ quadrilateral

☐ parallelogram

☐ rectangle

☐ square

3.

[shape: square]

☐ quadrilateral

☐ parallelogram

☐ rectangle

☐ square

4.

☐ quadrilateral

☐ parallelogram

☐ rectangle

☐ square

5.

☐ quadrilateral

☐ parallelogram

☐ rectangle

☐ square

6.

☐ quadrilateral

☐ parallelogram

☐ rectangle

☐ square

7. On the Back Draw a shape that is a parallelogram but *not* a rectangle.

Relate Different Quadrilaterals

For each description, write the correct shape name.

1. The shape has three corners and three

   sides. _____

2. The shape has four square corners and four

   equal sides. _____

3. Find the perimeter of this shape. Use a centimeter ruler.

   $P =$ _____ cm

4. Ring each pair of parallel lines.

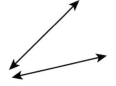 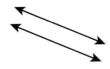 

5. Ring each parallelogram.

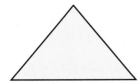   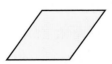

6. Draw two different parallelograms that will fit
   between these two lines.

   _____

   _____

Place a check mark beside each word that names the shape.

7.

☐ quadrilateral

☐ parallelogram

☐ rectangle

☐ square

8.

☐ quadrilateral

☐ parallelogram

☐ rectangle

☐ square

9.

☐ quadrilateral

☐ parallelogram

☐ rectangle

☐ square

10. Extended Response Marco says that all triangles have sides with equal lengths. Do you agree or disagree? Explain. Include pictures and words in your answer.

_____

_____

_____

_____

_____

Name _____

► **Write the Numbers 101 to 200**

1. Write the numbers going down to see the tens.

101	111								
102		122			152				
103						163			193
				144					
								185	
	116				156				
		128							
								189	
110	120			150		170			200

🡒 **2. On the Back** Show these numbers in as many ways as you can.

101   150   200

Ones, Tens, and Hundreds

Dear Family,

Your child is learning about place value and will use this knowledge of place value to add 2- and 3-digit numbers.

As we begin this unit, your child will show or represent numbers using drawings. Children have been representing numbers using drawings like this:

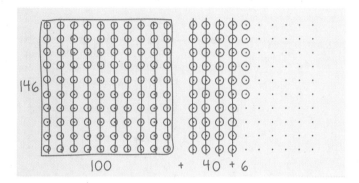

Then, they will begin to represent numbers using Quick Hundreds and Quick Tens.

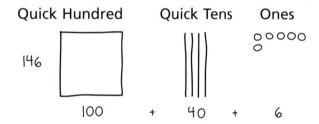

Try giving your child a 2- or 3-digit number and ask your child to make a drawing to represent that number.

Later in this unit, children will work on adding 2-digit numbers using the drawings to help them. They can make Proof Drawings with boxes, sticks, and circles to demonstrate how a new ten is formed from 10 ones.

$48 + 15 = \square$

Thank you. Please call or write if you have any questions.

Sincerely,
Your child's teacher

Estimada familia:

Su niño está aprendiendo a comprender el valor posicional y usará esta comprensión para sumar números de 2 y 3 dígitos.

Cuando comencemos con esta unidad su niño mostrará o representará números por medio de dibujos. Los estudiantes han estado representando números por medio de dibujos como éstos:

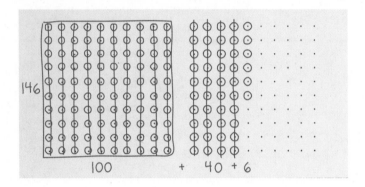

Luego, comenzarán a representar números por medio de "Centenas rápidas" y "Decenas rápidas".

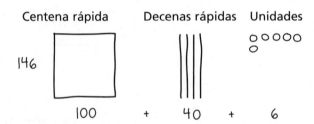

Dígale a su niño un número de 2 ó 3 dígitos. Pídale que haga un dibujo para representar ese número.

Luego, los niños trabajarán sumando números de 2 dígitos y usarán los dibujos como ayuda. Pueden hacer dibujos de prueba con cajas, palitos y círculos para demostrar cómo se forma una nueva decena a partir de 10 unidades.

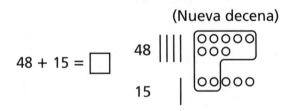

Gracias. Si tiene alguna pregunta, por favor comuníquese conmigo.

Atentamente,
El maestro de su niño

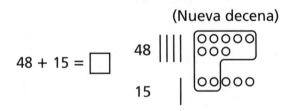

Ones, Tens, and Hundreds

► **Add Tens or Ones**

1. 10 + 20 = _____   70 + 20 = _____   60 + 30 = _____

   1 + 2 = _____   7 + 2 = _____   6 + 3 = _____

2. 20 + 70 = _____   30 + 50 = _____   40 + 50 = _____

   2 + 7 = _____   3 + 5 = _____   4 + 5 = _____

3. 30 + 60 = _____   20 + 80 = _____   50 + 40 = _____

   3 + 6 = _____   2 + 8 = _____   5 + 4 = _____

4. 50 + 50 = _____   80 + 20 = _____   40 + 60 = _____

   5 + 5 = _____   8 + 2 = _____   4 + 6 = _____

5. 90 + 10 = _____   90 + 20 = _____   40 + 30 = _____

   9 + 1 = _____   9 + 2 = _____   4 + 3 = _____

6. **On the Back** Show the number 158 in as many ways as you can.

Name

Draw Quick Tens and Quick Hundreds

Class Activity

Name _____

Vocabulary

hundreds
tens
ones

▶ **Hundreds, Tens, and Ones**

Draw these numbers using hundred boxes, sticks, and circles. Then write the **hundreds**, **tens**, and **ones**.

1. ☐ ○○○○○ ○	2.	3.
106	122	139
_100_ + _0_ + _6_	___ + ___ + ___	___ + ___ + ___

What number is shown?   H = Hundreds, T = Tens, O = Ones

4. ☐ |||| ○○○○○ ○○	5. ☐ |||||| || ○
_1_ H _4_ T _7_ O	___ H ___ T ___ O
_147_ = _100_ + _40_ + _7_	___ = ___ + ___ + ___
6. ☐ ||||| |	7. ☐ ||||| ||| ○○○○○ ○○○○
___ H ___ T ___ O	___ H ___ T ___ O
___ = ___ + ___ + ___	___ = ___ + ___ + ___

Name _____

Class Activity

Vocabulary

word name

▶ **Recognize Word Names for Numbers**

1 one	11 eleven	10 ten	100 one hundred
2 two	12 twelve	20 twenty	
3 three	13 thirteen	30 thirty	
4 four	14 fourteen	40 forty	
5 five	15 fifteen	50 fifty	
6 six	16 sixteen	60 sixty	
7 seven	17 seventeen	70 seventy	
8 eight	18 eighteen	80 eighty	
9 nine	19 nineteen	90 ninety	

Write the number.

1. thirty-five _____

2. seventy-two _____

3. fifty-four _____

4. eighty-nine _____

5. sixty-three _____

6. ninety-one _____

Write the word name.

7. 47 _____

8. 62 _____

9. 85 _____

10. 94 _____

11. 28 _____

12. 86 _____

Represent Write the word name and draw
Quick Tens and ones in the box.

13. 60 _____

14. 72 _____

Represent Numbers in Different Ways

Get 5 Dimes

Get 5 Dimes

Name _____

Class Activity

▶ **Solve and Discuss**

Add.

1. 48 + 7 = _____   2. 41 + 3 = _____   3. 84 + 5 = _____

4. 32 + 6 = _____   5. 59 + 4 = _____   6. 73 + 9 = _____

7. 24 + 6 = _____   8. 66 + 6 = _____   9. 37 + 5 = _____

10. 63 + 9 = _____   11. 89 + 4 = _____   12. 23 + 8 = _____

13. 20 + 30 = _____   20 + 80 = _____   60 + 40 = _____

2 + 3 = _____   2 + 8 = _____   6 + 4 = _____

14. 50 + 50 = _____   70 + 20 = _____   30 + 60 = _____

5 + 5 = _____   7 + 2 = _____   3 + 6 = _____

15. 90 + 10 = _____   50 + 30 = _____   40 + 30 = _____

9 + 1 = _____   5 + 3 = _____   4 + 3 = _____

16. **On the Back** Billy has 80 buttons. He gives
30 away. Sonya asks Billy for 60 buttons.
Does he have enough to give her?
Explain how you know.

Add 2-Digit and 1-Digit Numbers

Add 2-Digit and 1-Digit Numbers

Going Further

▶ Round 2-Digit Numbers

Use the number lines to round each number to the nearest ten.

1. 34 rounds down to _____   38 rounds up to _____

2. 36 rounds up to _____   49 rounds up to _____

3. 42 rounds down to _____   45 rounds up to _____

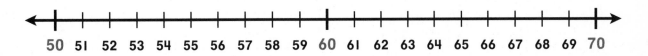

4. 58 rounds to _____   55 rounds to _____   51 rounds to _____

5. 69 rounds to _____   63 rounds to _____   53 rounds to _____

6. 56 rounds to _____   67 rounds to _____   65 rounds to _____

Logical Thinking Use the clues to find the number.

Clues:

7. • It rounds to 30.
   • The number of ones is greater than the number of tens.
   • It is greater than 30.

   What number is it? _____

Clues:

8. • It rounds to 40, and it is less than 40.
   • It is an even number.
   • The number of ones is double the number of tens.

   What number is it? _____

➡ 9. **On the Back** Write all of the numbers you can think of that round to 50. (Hint: Think about numbers less than 50 and numbers greater than 50.)

Name _____

Find Decade Partners

▶ **Story Problems with Groups of Ten**

Solve each story problem.

---

1. Remah has 34 stickers. Only 10 stickers fit on a page in her scrapbook. How many pages can she fill with stickers? How many stickers will be left over?

   [ ] pages   [ ] stickers left over

---

2. David has 42 beads. He wants to make some necklaces that take 10 beads each. How many necklaces can he make? How many beads will be left over?

   [ ] necklaces   [ ] beads left over

---

3. The team wants to buy T-shirts that cost 10 dollars each. They have 57 dollars. How many shirts can they buy? How many dollars will be left over?

   [ ] T-shirts   [ ] dollars left over

---

4. The store has 63 apples. Each basket can hold 10 apples. How many baskets can they fill with apples? How many apples will be left over?

   [ ] baskets   [ ] apples left over

Name _____

Going Further

► **Estimate with Ten-Benchmarks**

Ring a group of 10. Estimate how many in all.
Then count the exact number.

1.

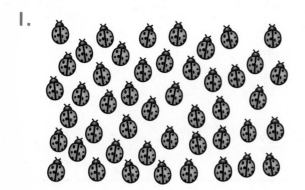

Estimate: about _____

Exact number: _____

2.

Estimate: about _____

Exact number: _____

3.

Estimate: about _____

Exact number: _____

4.

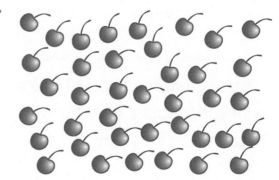

Estimate: about _____

Exact number: _____

5. **Create Your Own** On a separate piece of paper,
   draw as many circles as you wish. Give your
   drawing to a classmate. Then challenge your
   classmate to estimate how many circles are
   in your drawing.

Combine Ones, Tens, and Hundreds

Class Activity

▶ **The New Ten**

Solve each story problem.

1. Mr. Green put 56 red peppers in the vegetable bin. Mrs. Green put 28 yellow peppers in the bin. How many peppers did they put in the bin altogether?

☐ _____
label

2. Mrs. Green stacked 43 tomatoes. Mr. Green added 39 more. How many tomatoes are stacked now?

☐ _____
label

3. Mr. Green counted 65 cans. Mrs. Green counted 82 cans. How many cans did they count in all?

☐ _____
label

4. Mrs. Green counted 57 bags of beans. Mr. Green counted 71 bags of beans. How many bags of beans did they count in all?

☐ _____
label

5. **On the Back** Solve problem 4 in a different way.

　　　　　　　　　　　　　　　　　　　　　　　　Invent 2-Digit Addition **153**

Name

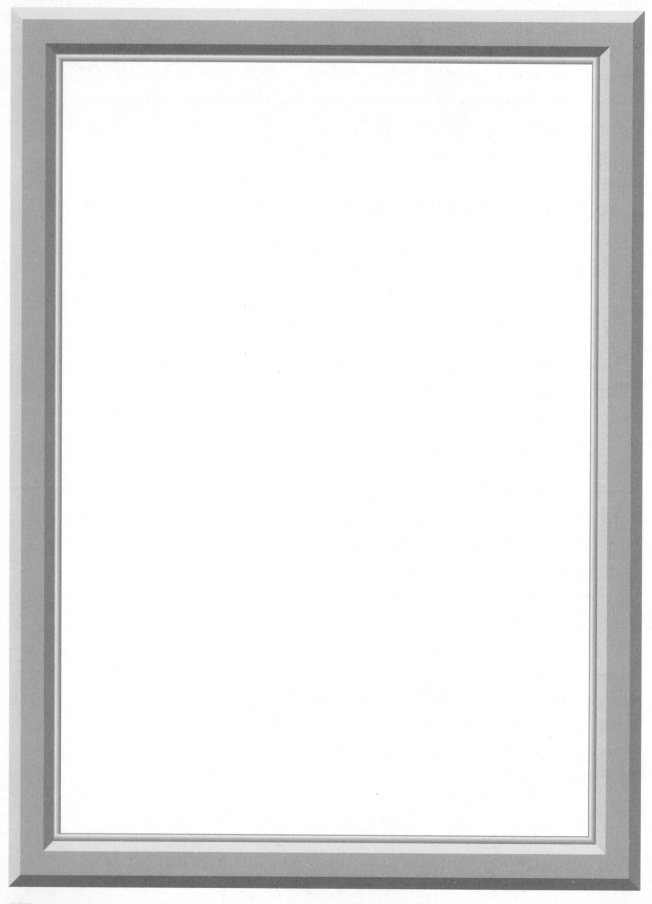

Invent 2-Digit Addition

Dear Family,

Your child is now learning how to add 2-digit numbers. Children will first do this with methods they invent themselves. Research has shown that children take pride in using their own methods.

Math Expressions then shows children two methods for 2-digit addition, but children may use any method that they understand, can explain, and can do fairly quickly. We will show these methods in class.

The "big mystery" in adding is making a new ten or a new hundred. Children can write this new group in several ways.

Show All Totals	New Groups Below
$\begin{array}{r} 45 \\ + 28 \\ \hline \end{array}$ Add tens. → 60 Add ones. → 13 $\overline{73}$ Find total tens. Find total ones. New ten	$\begin{array}{r} 45 \\ + 28 \\ + \\ \hline 73 \end{array}$ New ten Find total ones. (13) Write 3 and put the new ten in the tens column ready to add. Add the tens. (4 + 2 = 6, 6 + 1 = 7)

Children usually find it easier to write the new ten below because then they add the new ten last. They add 4 + 2 = 6 and then 6 + 1 = 7.

Traditionally, most children have learned to write the new ten above. With this method, you add 1 + 4 = 5 and then 5 + 2 = 7. This is more difficult for many children, but some children may still choose this method, particularly if they have been taught to do so previously.

Thank you for helping your child learn mathematics.

Sincerely,
Your child's teacher

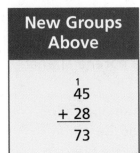

New Groups Above

$$\begin{array}{r} \overset{1}{4}5 \\ + 28 \\ \hline 73 \end{array}$$

Invent 2-Digit Addition **155**

Estimada familia:

Su niño está aprendiendo a sumar números de 2 dígitos. Los niños empezarán a hacer esto con métodos que ellos mismos inventen. Los estudios han demostrado que los niños se enorgullecen de usar sus propios métodos.

A continuación, *Math Expressions* muestra a los niños otros métodos para sumar números de 2 dígitos, pero ellos pueden usar cualquier método que comprendan, que puedan explicar y que puedan emplear rápidamente. Mostraremos en clase estos métodos.

El "misterio" en la suma de números de 2 dígitos por lo general requiere formar una nueva decena o una nueva centena. Los niños pueden anotar este nuevo grupo de varias maneras.

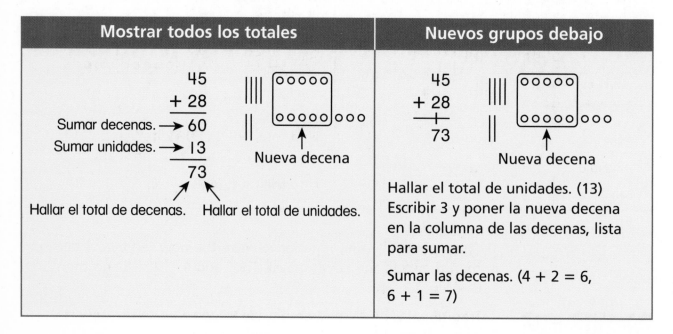

Mostrar todos los totales	Nuevos grupos debajo

Por lo general a los niños les resulta más fácil escribir la nueva decena debajo, porque entonces suman la nueva decena al final. Suman 4 + 2 = 6 y luego 6 + 1 = 7.

Tradicionalmente la mayoría de los estudiantes han aprendido a escribir la nueva decena arriba. Con este método, se suma 1 + 4 = 5 y luego 5 + 2 = 7. Para muchos niños este método resulta más difícil pero algunos siguen escogiéndolo, en especial si ya lo han aprendido.

Gracias por ayudar a su niño a aprender matemáticas.

Atentamente,
El maestro de su niño

Nuevos grupos arriba

$$\begin{array}{r} {\scriptstyle 1} \\ 45 \\ + 28 \\ \hline 73 \end{array}$$

Invent 2-Digit Addition

▶ **Show All Totals Method**

1. Mr. Green will order 25 jars of grape jelly and 48 jars of strawberry jelly. How many jars of jelly will he order?

☐ _____
   label

2. Mrs. Green ordered 65 pounds of bananas. That was not enough. So she ordered 29 more pounds. How many pounds did she order altogether?

☐ _____
   label

3. Mrs. Green ordered 78 pounds of white rice and 57 pounds of brown rice. How many pounds of rice did she order?

☐ _____
   label

4. Mr. Green ordered 49 jars of plain peanut butter and 86 jars of chunky peanut butter. How many jars of peanut butter did he order in all?

☐ _____
   label

5. **On the Back** Make a Proof Drawing for problem 4.

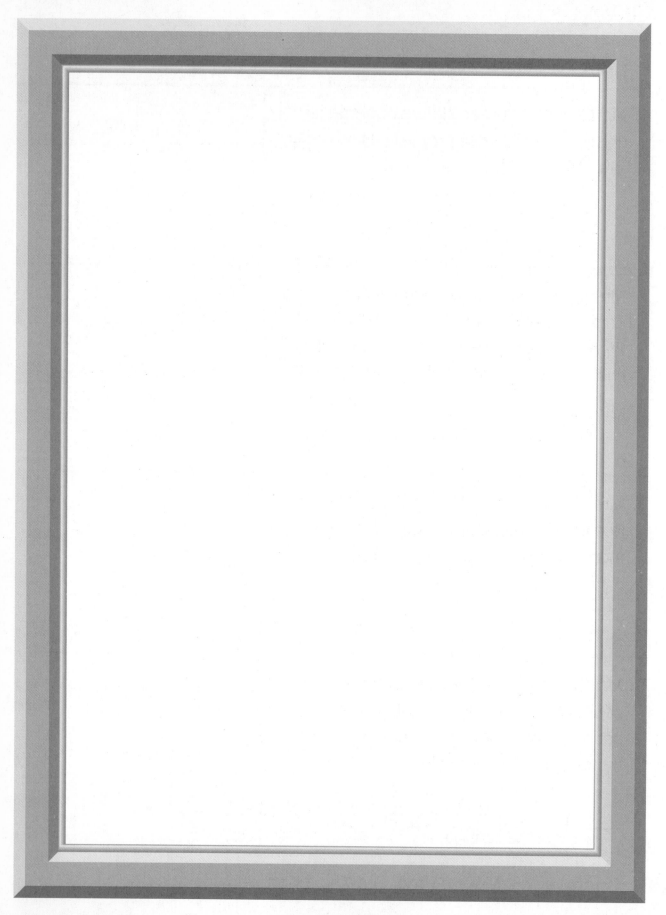

Addition – Show All Totals Method

Going Further

► **Introduce Estimating Sums**

Estimate the total.   41 + 25

You can use number lines and rounding to estimate a total.

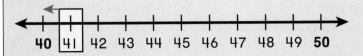

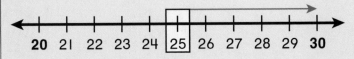

41 is closer to 40 than 50. Round down to 40.
25 is exactly in the middle of 20 and 30. Round up to 30.

40 + 30 = 70

► **Practice Estimating Sums**

Round each addend to the nearest ten. Estimate the total.

1. 13 + 28

_____ + _____ = _____

2. 46 + 29

_____ + _____ = _____

3. 45 + 38

_____ + _____ = _____

4. 24 + 31

_____ + _____ = _____

5. 42 + 15

_____ + _____ = _____

6. 49 + 46

_____ + _____ = _____

7. **On the Back** List all the numbers that round to 80.
   Draw a number line to help.

Addition – New Groups Below Method **159**

Addition – New Groups Below Method

▶ Practice Addition

Add. Use any method.

$$
\begin{array}{r} 86 \\ + 57 \\ \hline 130 \\ + 13 \\ \hline 143 \end{array}
\quad \text{or} \quad
\begin{array}{r} 86 \\ + 57 \\ \hline 143 \end{array}
$$

130 + 13 = 143

1.
$$\begin{array}{r} 39 \\ + 97 \\ \hline \end{array}$$
$$\begin{array}{r} 83 \\ + 39 \\ \hline \end{array}$$
$$\begin{array}{r} 61 \\ + 37 \\ \hline \end{array}$$
$$\begin{array}{r} 45 \\ + 47 \\ \hline \end{array}$$

2.
$$\begin{array}{r} 58 \\ + 87 \\ \hline \end{array}$$
$$\begin{array}{r} 72 \\ + 37 \\ \hline \end{array}$$
$$\begin{array}{r} 53 \\ + 21 \\ \hline \end{array}$$
$$\begin{array}{r} 86 \\ + 79 \\ \hline \end{array}$$

3.
$$\begin{array}{r} 49 \\ + 85 \\ \hline \end{array}$$
$$\begin{array}{r} 94 \\ + 52 \\ \hline \end{array}$$
$$\begin{array}{r} 66 \\ + 27 \\ \hline \end{array}$$
$$\begin{array}{r} 78 \\ + 63 \\ \hline \end{array}$$

Toy	Price
ball	58¢
marbles	65¢
top	26¢
train	52¢
truck	48¢

4. On the Back Write and solve your own word problem using the information in the table.

Name _____

_____

_____

_____

_____

_____

_____

_____

_____

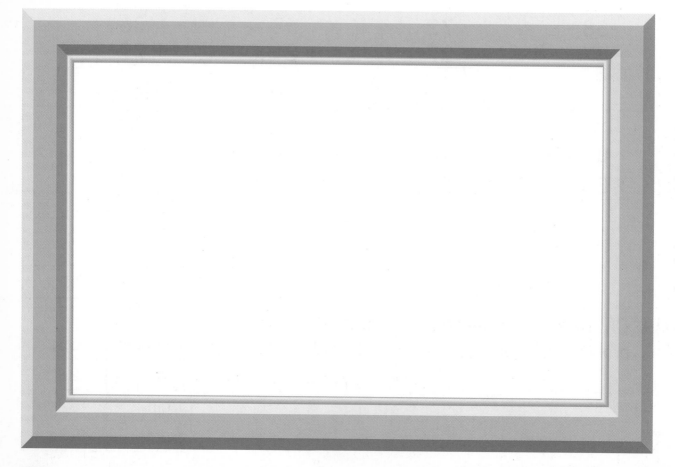

Practice Addition with Totals Over 100

Class Activity

Name

▶ **Addition Sprint**

5 + 7 =	9 + 6 =	7 + 6 =
4 + 8 =	7 + 8 =	4 + 6 =
3 + 9 =	9 + 7 =	0 + 7 =
7 + 5 =	9 + 2 =	4 + 9 =
4 + 5 =	5 + 2 =	6 + 8 =
8 + 4 =	6 + 4 =	8 + 5 =
8 + 6 =	8 + 7 =	6 + 1 =
6 + 9 =	5 + 5 =	5 + 4 =
9 + 9 =	1 + 9 =	7 + 4 =
6 + 3 =	7 + 9 =	3 + 6 =
9 + 0 =	4 + 7 =	9 + 4 =
7 + 7 =	8 + 8 =	5 + 8 =
9 + 1 =	6 + 6 =	3 + 4 =
8 + 9 =	3 + 5 =	6 + 7 =
2 + 5 =	9 + 3 =	1 + 6 =
3 + 9 =	2 + 9 =	5 + 6 =
2 + 7 =	2 + 6 =	5 + 5 =
9 + 4 =	5 + 9 =	6 + 8 =
2 + 8 =	8 + 2 =	4 + 4 =
0 + 8 =	9 + 8 =	1 + 8 =
8 + 3 =	6 + 5 =	6 + 7 =

Choose an Addition Method

Class Activity

Name _____

▶ **Perimeter at the Grocery Store**

Choose a method to solve the **perimeter** problems.
Does your method work for all of them? Be ready
to explain your method to the class.

1. Someone broke a jug of milk in the store.
   Mr. Green cleaned it up. Then he blocked
   off the wet spot with tape. How long was
   the tape?

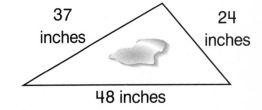

37 inches   24 inches

48 inches

☐ _____
    label

2. Mrs. Chang wants to decorate the table she
   uses for free food samples. She wants to put
   gold trim around the top of the table. How
   much trim will she need?

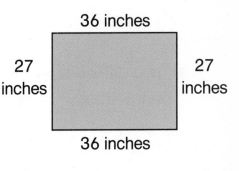

36 inches

27 inches   27 inches

36 inches

☐ _____
    label

3. Here is the route a customer took while
   shopping at the store. How far did the
   customer walk altogether?

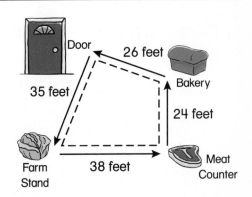

Door   26 feet   Bakery

35 feet   24 feet

Farm Stand   38 feet   Meat Counter

☐ _____
    label

Name

Going Further

▶ Find the Different Shapes

1. Draw two different rectangles with perimeters of 12 units.

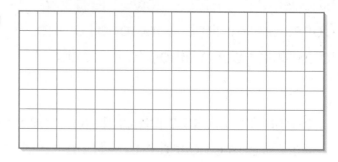

2. Draw two different rectangles with perimeters of 8 units.

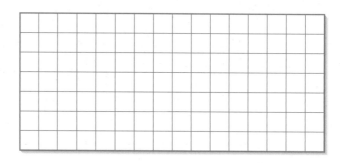

3. Draw two different rectangles with perimeters of 14 units.

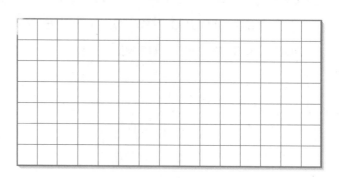

4. Draw 2 different rectangles with perimeters of 10 units.

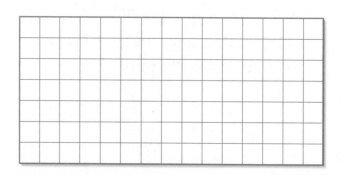

2-Digit Addition in Perimeter Problems

Dollar Bills   Cut along the dotted lines.

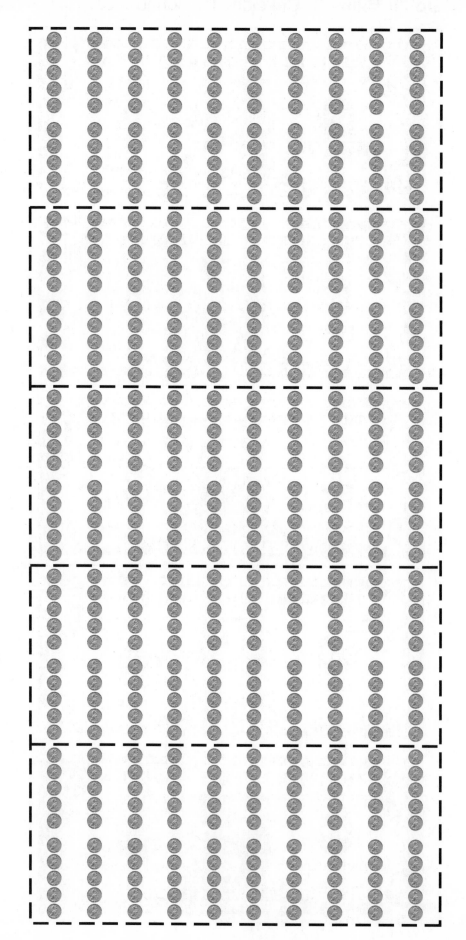

Dollar Bills

Class Activity

Name _____

▶ **The Farm Stand**

Potatoes 65¢	Corn 56¢	Bananas 89¢	Peaches 77¢
Radishes 76¢	Lemons 88¢	Celery 57¢	Peppers 78¢
Mushrooms 67¢	Carrots 86¢	Tomatoes 97¢	Grapes 98¢
Watermelon 59¢	Oranges 68¢	Raspberries 99¢	Green Beans 87¢

➡ **On the Back** Choose two items. Find the exact amount of money needed to buy the items. Show how you found the answer. Then draw the coins that you could use to buy the items.

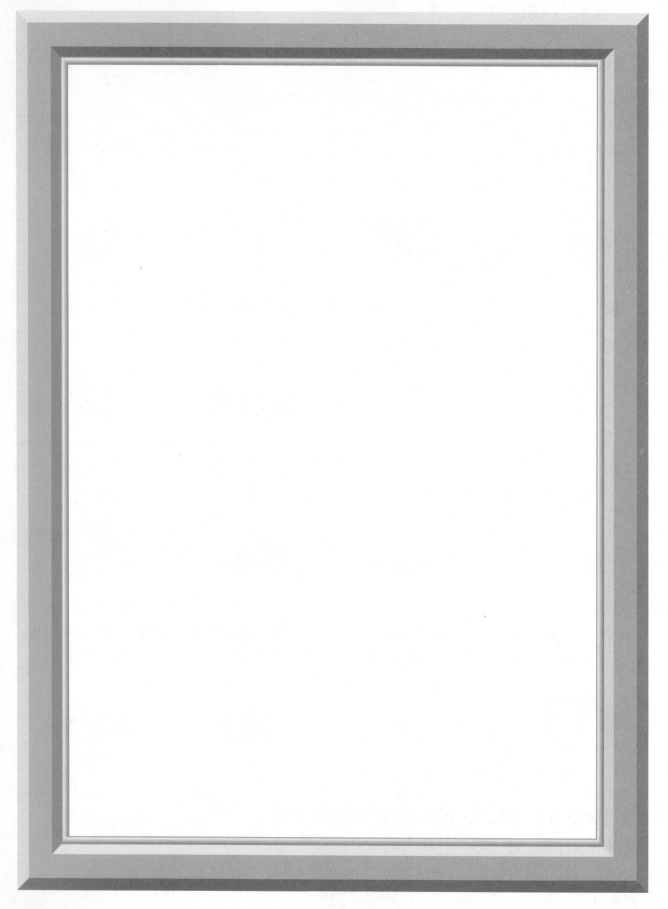

Buy with Pennies and Dimes

Class Activity

► **How Much Money?**

Under the coins, write the total amount of money so far.
The first one is done for you.

1. 10¢   10¢   1¢

   <u>10¢</u> <u>20¢</u> <u>21¢</u>

2. 10¢   10¢   10¢   5¢   1¢   1¢

   _____ _____ _____ _____ _____ _____

3. 10¢   10¢   10¢   10¢   5¢   1¢   1¢   1¢

   _____

4. 10¢   10¢   10¢   10¢   10¢   10¢   10¢   5¢   1¢

   ___ ___ ___ ___ ___ ___ ___ ___ ___

5. Draw the coins you could use to show 54¢.
   Use ⑩, ⑤, and ①.

Buy with Pennies, Nickels, and Dimes **171**

Class Activity

Name

▶ **The Snack Bar**

Choose two items. On a separate piece of paper, show
the exact amount of money needed to buy the items.

Banana 56¢	Muffin 87¢	Milk 77¢	Apple 58¢
Pretzels 68¢	Granola Bar 98¢	Sandwich 99¢	Taco 95¢
Yogurt 75¢	Pickle 57¢	Orange Juice 79¢	Orange 88¢
Pasta 65¢	Soup 78¢	Nuts 89¢	Peach 67¢

Buy with Pennies, Nickels, and Dimes

▶ **Alphabet Addition**

A	B	C	D	E	F	G	H	I	J	K	L	M
1	2	3	4	5	6	7	8	9	10	11	12	13

N	O	P	Q	R	S	T	U	V	W	X	Y	Z
14	15	16	17	18	19	20	21	22	23	24	25	26

1. Write your first name in the top row of boxes. Put one letter in each box.

2. Now look up the number that goes with each letter of your name. Write them in the bottom row of boxes. Add up all the numbers. What is the total?

Here's an example. It is for the name "Terry."

T	E	R	R	Y					
20	5	18	18	25					

TERRY = 20 + 5 + 18 + 18 + 25 = 86

Try this with other names. Try it with words too.

3. **On the Back** Find a word with a total greater than 100.

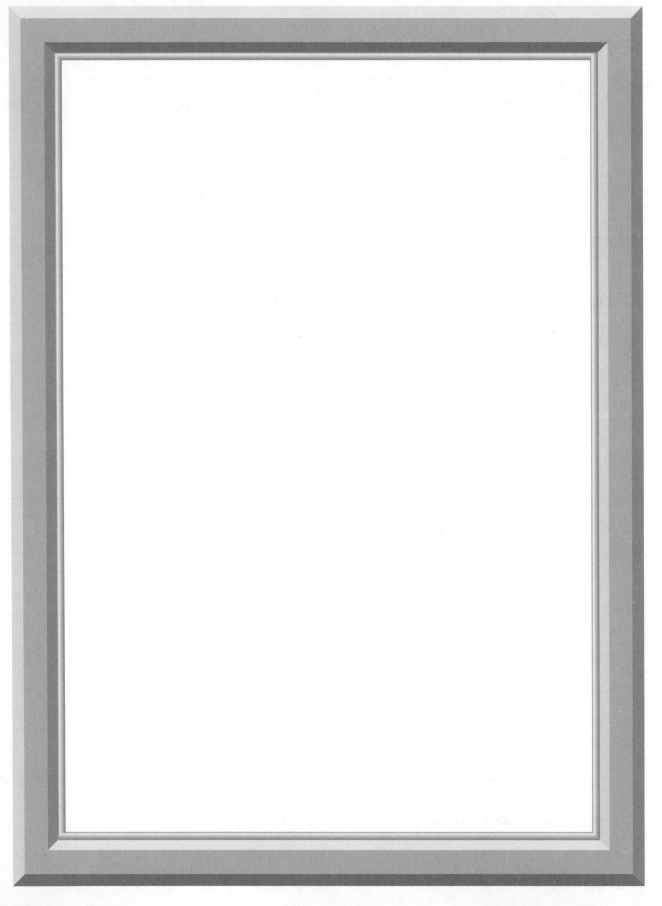

Skip-Counting and Addition Practice

Draw each number using hundred boxes, ten sticks, and circles.

1. 148

2. 163

What number is shown?
Write the number and write the number in words.

3. ☐ ‖ ∘∘∘∘

_____

_____

4. ☐ ∘∘∘

_____

_____

Add.

5. 83
   + 6

6. 80
   + 10

7. 60
   + 40

Add.

8. 75 + 24 = _____

9. 86 + 32 = _____

10. 59 + 37 = _____

11. 78 + 95 = _____

Solve each story problem.   Show your work.

12. Arnez and Jada counted insects in the
park. Arnez counted 56 ants. Jada
counted 37 ladybugs. How many insects
did they count altogether?

[ ] _____
       label

13. Terrel scored 88 points in a computer
game. He scored 43 points in the next
game. How many points did he score
altogether?

[ ] _____
       label

Test

Name _____

Under the coins write the total amount of money so far.

14.   10¢   10¢   10¢   5¢   1¢   1¢   1¢

   10¢   20¢   _____   _____   _____   _____

15.   10¢   10¢   5¢   5¢   5¢   5¢   1¢

   10¢   20¢   _____   _____   _____   _____

Continue each number sequence.
Write the rule.

16. 16, 24, 32, _____, _____, _____   Rule: *n* _____

17. 48, 43, 38, _____, _____, _____   Rule: *n* _____

18. 26, 32, 38, _____, _____, _____   Rule: *n* _____

19. 57, 54, 51, _____, _____, _____   Rule: *n* _____

20. **Extended Response** Explain how you find the
total of 29 and 84. Then make a Proof Drawing.

_____

_____

_____

_____

_____

_____

Class Activity

Name _____

Vocabulary

clock   minute hand
analog clock   hour hand

► **Features of Clocks**

Clocks are tools that we use to measure time.

1. Describe some clocks that you have seen.

_____

_____

Place the missing numbers on the **analog clocks**.

2.

3.

4.

An analog clock has a long hand that is the **minute hand**
and a short hand that is the **hour hand**.
Ring the hour hand on the clocks.

5.

6.

7.

Ring the minute hand on the clocks.

8.

9.

10.

Class Activity

▶ **Times of Daily Activities**

> We use **A.M.** for the hours after 12 midnight and before 12 noon.
>   9:00 A.M. is 9 o'clock in the morning.
> We use **P.M.** for the hours after 12 noon and before 12 midnight.
>   9:00 P.M. is 9 o'clock in the evening.

11. Complete the chart. For each time listed, write
    whether it is dark or light outside; whether it is
    morning, afternoon, or evening; and an activity
    you might be doing at that time.

Time	Sunlight	Part of the Day	Activity
4:00 A.M.	dark	very early morning	sleeping
12 noon			
9:00 P.M.			

For each activity, ring the most appropriate time.

12. Brush your teeth in the morning.

     1:30 P.M.   3:00 P.M.   7:30 A.M.

13. Eat dinner at night.

     5:00 A.M.   12:00 noon   6:00 P.M.

Class Activity

▶ **Make a Clock**

Attach the clock hands using a prong fastener.

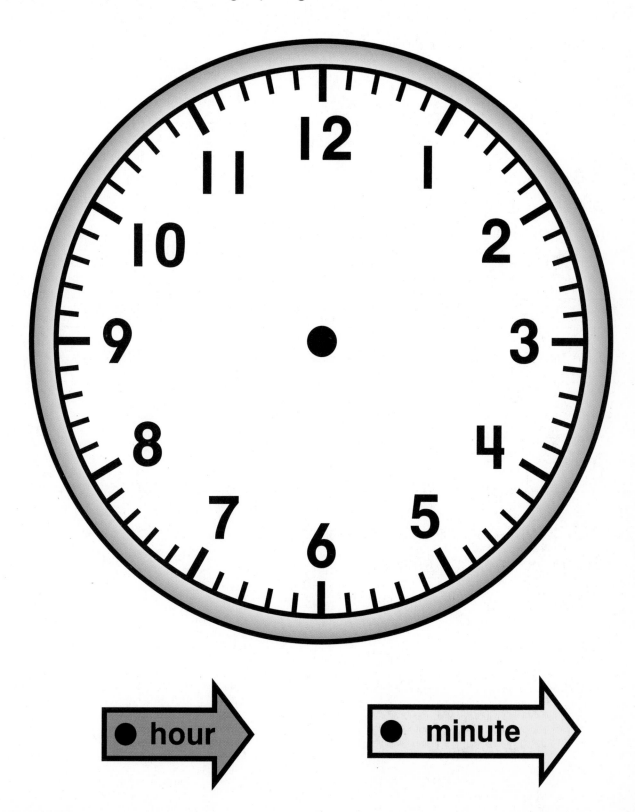

Hours on the Clock

Vocabulary

digital clock

▶ **Write Time**

On a **digital clock**, the number on the left shows the hour and the number on the right shows the minutes after the hour.

hour   minutes

Write each time in two different ways.

12.

o'clock
_____

13.

o'clock
_____

14.

_____

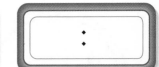

15.

_____

16.

_____

17.

_____

18.

_____

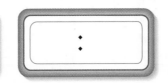

19.

_____

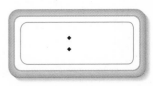

Class Activity

▶ **Draw Clock Hands**

Draw the hands on each analog clock and write the time on each digital clock below.

20.

7 o'clock

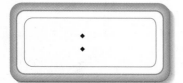

21.

11 o'clock

22.

2 o'clock

23.

3 o'clock

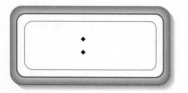

24.

5 o'clock

25.

10 o'clock

Hours on the Clock

Dear Family,

Your child is beginning a new unit on time. This topic is directly connected to home and community and involves skills your child will use often in everyday situations.

You can help your child link the time concepts learned in school with the real world.

Together, look for clocks in your home. You might search for watches, alarm clocks, digital clocks, and clocks on appliances.

Talk about time throughout your family's day. For example, you can point to the clock during breakfast and say, "We usually eat breakfast at this time. It is 7:30 A.M."

Encourage your child to estimate the length of time he or she spends on specific activities like brushing teeth, sleeping, or traveling to school.

In this unit, your child will first learn to tell time to the hour. Your child will practice writing the time shown on a clock in two different ways.

| 4 o'clock | 1 o'clock | 11 o'clock |
| 4:00 | 1:00 | 11:00 |

If you have any questions or comments, please call or write to me. Thank you.

Sincerely,
Your child's teacher

Estimada familia:

Su niño está empezando una unidad sobre la hora. Este tema está directamente conectado con el hogar y la comunidad, y requiere destrezas que su niño usará a menudo en situaciones de la vida diaria.

Puede ayudar a su niño a que conecte los conceptos relacionados con la hora que aprendió en la escuela con el mundo real.

Busquen juntos relojes en la casa. Puede buscar relojes de pulsera, relojes con alarma, relojes digitales y relojes que estén en los electrodomésticos.

Durante un día en familia, hablen de la hora. Por ejemplo, puede señalar un reloj durante el desayuno y decir "Generalmente desayunamos a esta hora. Son las 7:30 a.m."

Anime a su niño a estimar la cantidad de tiempo que pasa haciendo determinadas actividades como lavarse los dientes, dormir o ir a la escuela.

En esta unidad su niño aprenderá primero a decir la hora en punto. Su niño practicará cómo escribir la hora de dos maneras.

Si tiene alguna pregunta o algún inconveniente, por favor comuníquese conmigo. Gracias.

Atentamente,
El maestro de su niño

Class Activity

Name _____

▶ **5-Minute Intervals**

1. Count by 5s around the clock.

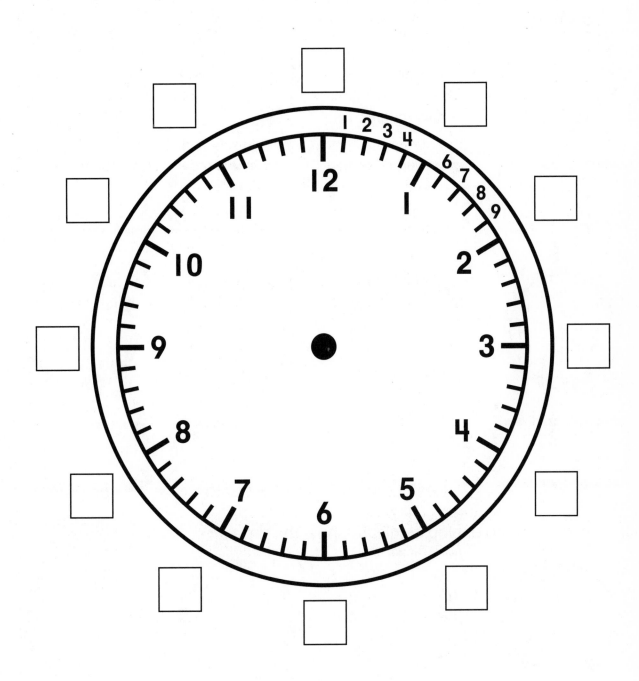

Class Activity

Name _____

▶ **Read and Show Time to 5 Minutes**

Write the time on the digital clocks.

2.

3.

4.

5.

6.

7.

8.

9.

Draw hands on the analog clocks to show the time.

10.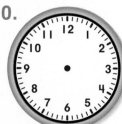

11.

12.

13.

10:35

9:20

2:25

4:50

Hours and Minutes

▶ **More on Time to 5 Minutes**

Write the time on each digital clock.

1.

[:]

2.

[:]

3.

[:]

4.

[:]

Draw hands on each clock to show the time.

5.

7:05

6.

3:30

7.

5:50

8.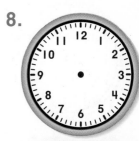

8:00

9.

10:15

10.

12:25

11.

3:55

12.

4:30

Class Activity

Name _____

▶ Read and Show Time to 1 Minute

Write the time on each digital clock.

13.

[___ : ___]

14.

[___ : ___]

15.

[___ : ___]

Draw hands on each clock to show the time.

16.

`10:17`

17.

`3:52`

18.

`7:38`

▶ Time Before and After the Hour

Write the time.

19.

_____ minutes before _____

_____ minutes after _____

20.

_____ minutes before _____

_____ minutes after _____

More on Telling Time

Class Activity

Name _____

Vocabulary

month
calendar

▶ **Make a Calendar**

Print the name of the current **month** at the top of the
calendar. Place a I under the first day of the month.
Then fill in the numbers for the rest of the month
across each row.

Month of _____

Sunday	Monday	Tuesday	Wednesday	Thursday	Friday	Saturday

Class Activity

▶ Learn About Months

This chart shows the months in a year.

1. Write the number of days in each month.

January	February	March	April
May	June	July	August
September	October	November	December

Answer the questions below about the months of the year.

2. How many months are in 1 year? _____

3. What is the name of the seventh month? _____

4. What month comes 5 months after February? _____

5. What month comes 6 months before November? _____

6. What month comes 4 months after November? _____

List the months.

7. Months with 30 days: _____ _____

   _____ _____

8. Months with 31 days: _____ _____ _____

   _____ _____ _____ _____

9. Which month has fewer than 30 days? _____

Write each date. Use a calendar.

10. One week after June 16 is _____.

11. One week after September 24 is _____.

Class Activity

▶ **Continue the Pattern**

Complete each table for exercises 12–14.

12.

Number of Weeks	Number of Days
1	7
2	14
3	
4	
5	
6	
7	

13.

Number of Years	Number of Months
1	12
2	24
3	36
4	
5	
6	
7	

14.

Number of Weeks	Number of School Days
1	5
2	10
3	
4	
5	
6	
7	

15. How many days are in 11 weeks?

_____

How many months are in 8 years?

_____

How many school days are in

9 weeks? _____

Class Activity

▶ **Solve Problems with Patterns**

Complete the table to solve each problem.

16. Jamil saves $3 every week from completing after-school chores. How much money has he saved after 5 weeks?

Weeks	1	2	3	4	5
Savings (dollars)					

_____ dollars

17. Pedro spends 6 hours in school each day. How many hours does he spend in school each week?

Days	1	2	3	4	5
Hours					

_____ hours

18. Celia puts 10¢ in a piggy bank each day. How much money does she have in her piggy bank after 7 days?

Days	1	2	3	4	5	6	7
Total (cents)							

_____ cents

19. Matthew travels 9 miles each school day. How far does he travel in 5 school days?

Days	1	2	3	4	5
Distance (miles)					

_____ miles

Write the time on each digital clock.

1.

[:]

2.

[:]

3.

[:]

4.

[:]

5. Draw hands on the analog clock to show the time.

Write each time as before the hour and after the hour.

6.

7.

_____ minutes before _____   _____ minutes before _____

_____ minutes after _____   _____ minutes after _____

For each activity, ring the most appropriate time.

8. Wake up in the morning.

  7:00 P.M.   1:00 P.M.   6:30 A.M.

9. Go to the beach in the afternoon.

  9:00 A.M.   2:00 P.M.   11:00 P.M.

For each activity, ring the unit of time you would use.

10. Run around the school field seven times.

  months   days   hours   minutes

11. Go on a camping trip.

  days   hours   minutes   seconds

Write the start time and end time. Then find how much time passed.

12.

Start Time	End Time	How long did it take?
_____ P.M.	_____ P.M.	_____

13.

Start Time	End Time	How long did it take?
_____ A.M.	_____ A.M.	_____

14. Complete the table.

Number of Weeks	Number of Days
1	7
2	
3	
4	28
5	
6	
7	

January

S	M	T	W	TH	F	S
1	2	3	4	5	6	7
8	9	10	11	12	13	14
15	16	17	18	19	20	21
22	23	24	25	26	27	28
29	30	31				

February

S	M	T	W	TH	F	S
				1	2	3	4
5	6	7	8	9	10	11
12	13	14	15	16	17	18
19	20	21	22	23	24	25
26	27	28				

March

S	M	T	W	TH	F	S
			1	2	3	4
5	6	7	8	9	10	11
12	13	14	15	16	17	18
19	20	21	22	23	24	25
26	27	28	29	30	31	

April

S	M	T	W	TH	F	S
						1
2	3	4	5	6	7	8
9	10	11	12	13	14	15
16	17	18	19	20	21	22
23	24	25	26	27	28	29
30						

May

S	M	T	W	TH	F	S
	1	2	3	4	5	6
7	8	9	10	11	12	13
14	15	16	17	18	19	20
21	22	23	24	25	26	27
28	29	30	31			

June

S	M	T	W	TH	F	S
				1	2	3
4	5	6	7	8	9	10
11	12	13	14	15	16	17
18	19	20	21	22	23	24
25	26	27	28	29	30	

July

S	M	T	W	TH	F	S
						1
2	3	4	5	6	7	8
9	10	11	12	13	14	15
16	17	18	19	20	21	22
23	24	25	26	27	28	29
30	31					

August

S	M	T	W	TH	F	S
		1	2	3	4	5
6	7	8	9	10	11	12
13	14	15	16	17	18	19
20	21	22	23	24	25	26
27	28	29	30	31		

September

S	M	T	W	TH	F	S
					1	2
3	4	5	6	7	8	9
10	11	12	13	14	15	16
17	18	19	20	21	22	23
24	25	26	27	28	29	30

October

S	M	T	W	TH	F	S
1	2	3	4	5	6	7
8	9	10	11	12	13	14
15	16	17	18	19	20	21
22	23	24	25	26	27	28
29	30	31				

November

S	M	T	W	TH	F	S
			1	2	3	4
5	6	7	8	9	10	11
12	13	14	15	16	17	18
19	20	21	22	23	24	25
26	27	28	29	30		

December

S	M	T	W	TH	F	S
					1	2
3	4	5	6	7	8	9
10	11	12	13	14	15	16
17	18	19	20	21	22	23
24	25	26	27	28	29	30
31						

Use the calendar to answer questions 15–19.

15. Which day of the week is the seventeenth of September? _____

16. Which month immediately follows October? _____

17. Which months only have 30 days?

_____ _____ _____ _____

18. Name the seventh month. _____

19. Which day of the week is the fifth of July? _____

20. **Extended Response** Explain how you can use skip counting to find the time shown on the clock.

_____

_____

_____

Glossary

add

$$4 + 2 = 6$$

addend

$$5 + 6 = 11$$

addends

Adding Up Method (for Subtraction)

$$
\begin{array}{r}
144 \\
-\ 68 \\
\hline
76
\end{array}
$$

$$68 + 2 = 70$$
$$70 + 30 = 100$$
$$100 + 44 = 144$$
$$\boxed{76}$$

after

98, 99

99 is after 98.

A.M.

The hours between midnight and noon.

angle

These are angles.

area

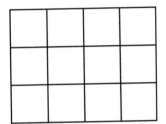

Area = 12 square units

You can find the area of a figure by covering it with square units and counting them.

array

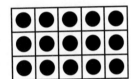

This picture shows a 3 × 5 array.

bar graph

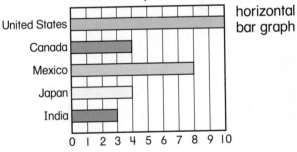

Coins in My Collection

horizontal bar graph

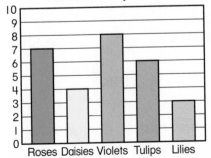

Flowers in My Garden

vertical bar graph

Glossary (Continued)

before

31, 32

31 is before 32.

cent

front   back

1 cent or 1¢ or $0.01

between

81, 82, 83

82 is between 81 and 83.

centimeter (cm)

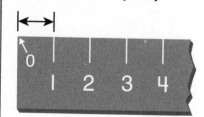

break-apart

You can break apart a larger number to get two smaller amounts called break-aparts.

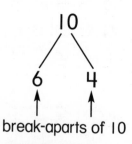

break-aparts of 10

C

certain

You are certain to choose a black button from the jar.

calendar

March						
February						
January						
Sun	Mon	Tues	Wed	Thurs	Fri	Sat
1	2	3	4	5	6	7
8	9	10	11	12	13	14
15	16	17	18	19	20	21
22	23	24	25	26	27	28
29	30	31				

change minus problem

Sarah had 12 books.
Then she loaned her friend 9 books.
How many books does Sarah have now?

$$12 - 9 = \boxed{3}$$

had   loaned   now

Any number may be unknown.

capacity

Capacity is how much a container holds.
This container holds 1 quart of milk.

change plus problem

Alvin had 9 toy cars.
Then he got 3 more.
How many toy cars does he have now?

9 + 3 = $\boxed{12}$

had   got   now

Any number may be unknown.

circle graph

Animals at Grasslands Nature Park

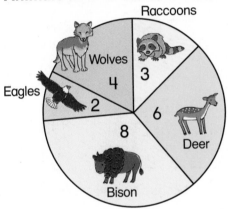

clock

analog clock

digital clock

collection problem

Jason put 8 large plates and 4 small plates on the table. How many plates are on the table altogether?

8 + 4 = $\boxed{12}$

large   small   altogether

comparison problem

Joe has 6 roses. Sasha has 9 roses.
How many more roses does Sasha have than Joe?

J   S

6 + ☐ = 9

9 − 6 = $\boxed{3}$

S   J

cone

congruent

These are congruent figures.

These are not congruent figures.

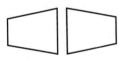

Congruent figures have the same size and shape.

Glossary (Continued)

count all

$$5 + 3 = \square$$

1 2 3 4 5 6 7 8

● ● ● ● ● | ● ● ●

$$5 + 3 = \boxed{8}$$

count by/count-bys

I can count by 2s.

2, 4, 6, 8, 10, 12, 14, 16, 18, and 20 are 2s count-bys.

count on

$$5 + 3 = \boxed{8}$$

$$5 + \boxed{3} = 8$$

$$8 - 5 = \boxed{3}$$

Already 5

cube

cylinder

D

data

	Hamsters	Mice
Kendra	5	8
Scott	2	9
Ida	7	3

data

The data in the table show how many hamsters and how many mice each child has.

day

November						
Sun	Mon	Tues	Wed	Thurs	Fri	Sat
	1	2	3	4	5	6
7	8	9	10	11	12	13
14	15	16	17	18	19	20
21	22	23	24	25	26	27
28	39	30				

November has 30 days. Each day has 24 hours.

decade numbers

10, 20, 30, 40, 50, 60, 70, 80, 90

decade partners

100
/ \
20   80

20 and 80 are decade partners of 100.

decimal point

$4.25

↑

decimal point

decimeter (dm)

decimeter

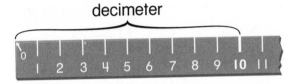

10 centimeters = 1 decimeter
(not drawn to scale)

denominator

$\frac{3}{4}$ ← denominator

The number of equal parts into which the 1 whole is divided.

diagonal

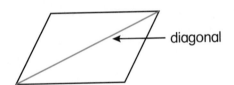

diagonal

difference

11 − 3 = 8

$$\begin{array}{r} 11 \\ -\ 3 \\ \hline 8 \end{array}$$

difference → 8

digits

0, 1, 2, 3, 4, 5, 6, 7, 8, 9

dime

front   back

10 cents or 10¢ or $0.10

dollar

100 cents or

100¢ or $1.00

front

back

dollar sign

$4.25
↑
dollar sign

doubles

Both addends (or partners) are the same.

4 + 4 = 8

doubles minus 1

7 + 7 = 14, so

7 + 6 = 13, 1 less than 14.

doubles plus 1

6 + 6 = 12, so

6 + 7 = 13, 1 more than 12.

Glossary (Continued)

E

edge

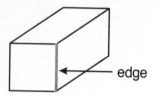

edge

equal shares

Maria and Rachel have equal shares of pennies.

equal to

5 + 3 = 8

5 plus 3 is equal to 8.

equation

4 + 3 = 7   7 = 4 + 3

9 − 5 = 4   4 + 5 = 8 + 1

An equation must have an = sign.

equation chain

3 + 4 = 5 + 2 = 8 − 1 = 7

estimate

An estimate is a number that is close to an exact amount.

$$28 \longrightarrow 30$$
$$+\ 23 \longrightarrow +\ 20$$
$$\overline{\ \ 50}$$

You can estimate a sum.

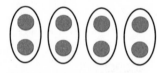

about 10

You can estimate the number of objects in a set.

even number

A number is even if you can make groups of 2 and have none left over.

8 is an even number.

exact change

I will pay with 4 dimes and 3 pennies. That is the exact change. I won't get any money back.

Expanded Method (for Addition)

$$78 = 70 + 8$$
$$+ 57 = 50 + 7$$
$$\overline{120 + 15 = 135}$$

Expanded Method (for Subtraction)

$$\begin{array}{r}
64 = \overset{50}{\cancel{60}} + \overset{14}{\cancel{4}} \\
-\ 28 = 20 + 8 \\
\hline
30 + 6 = 36
\end{array}$$

expanded number

$$283 = 200 + 80 + 3$$

F

face

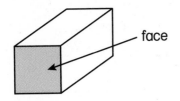

face

fair shares

fewer

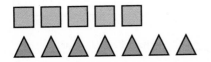

There are fewer ▢ than ▲.

flip

You can **flip** a figure over a **horizontal line**.

You can **flip** a figure over a **vertical line**.

foot (ft)

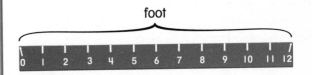

foot

12 inches = 1 foot
(not drawn to scale)

fourth

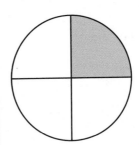

$\frac{1}{4}$ (one fourth) of the circle is shaded.

fraction

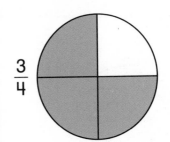

$\frac{3}{4}$

The fraction $\frac{3}{4}$ shows that 3 of 4 equal parts are shaded.

$$\frac{3}{4} = \frac{1}{4} + \frac{1}{4} + \frac{1}{4}$$

Glossary (Continued)

front-end estimation

$$
\begin{array}{r}
③4 \longrightarrow 30 \\
+①5 \longrightarrow + 10 \\
\hline
40
\end{array}
$$

function table

Add 3.	
0	3
1	4
2	5
3	6

G

greater than

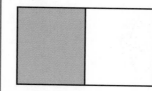

$$34 > 25$$

34 is greater than 25.

greatest

25   41   63

63 is the greatest number.

group name

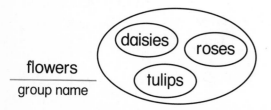

flowers
_____
group name

H

half

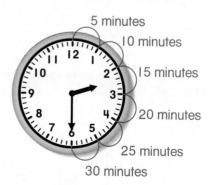

$\frac{1}{2}$ (one half) of the rectangle is shaded.

half-hour

5 minutes
10 minutes
15 minutes
20 minutes
25 minutes
30 minutes

30 minutes = 1 half-hour

hidden information

Heather bought a dozen eggs. She used 7 of them to make breakfast. How many eggs does she have left?

$12 - 7 = \boxed{5}$

The hidden information is that a dozen means 12.

horizontal

$4 + 5 = 9$

horizontal form   horizontal line

hour

60 minutes = 1 hour

hour hand

hour hand

hundreds

3 hundreds

347 has 3 hundreds.

↑
hundreds

I

impossible

It is impossible to choose a white button from this jar.

inch (in.)

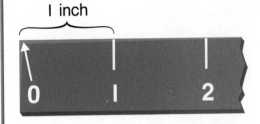

1 inch

K

key

Apples Bought

Red	
Green	
Yellow	

Key: Each 🍎 stands for 2 apples.

L

least

14   7   63

7 is the least number.

length

The length of the pencil is about 17 cm.

Glossary (Continued)

less likely

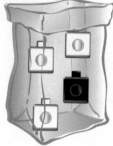

It is less likely that I will choose a black cube than a white cube if I choose a cube without looking.

less than

$$45 < 46$$

45 is less than 46.

line

line of symmetry

line of symmetry

line segment

M

Make a Ten

$$8 + 6 = \square$$

8 •• | ••••

$$10 + 4 = 14,$$
$$\text{so } 8 + 6 = 14$$

make change

Sellers make change when they give back money when a buyer pays too much.

mass

The mass of this bag of salt is 3 kg.

matching drawing

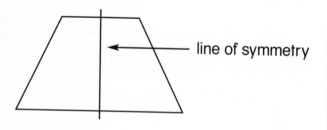

fewer

more

Math Mountain

sum

9 ← total

partner → 7   2 ← partner

addend   addend

measure

You measure to find the length, weight, mass, capacity, volume, or temperature of an object. You find how many units.

meter(m)

100 centimeters = 1 meter
(not drawn to scale)

midpoint

midpoint

The point exactly halfway between the ends of a line segment is the midpoint.

minus

$$8 - 3 = 5$$

$$\begin{array}{r} 8 \\ -\ 3 \\ \hline 5 \end{array}$$

8 minus 3 equals 5.

minute

I minute

60 seconds = 1 minute

minute hand

minute hand: points to the minutes

money string

$1.00 = 25¢ + 25¢ + 25¢ + 10¢ + 10¢ + 5¢

month

June						
Sun	Mon	Tues	Wed	Thurs	Fri	Sat
				1	2	3
4	5	6	7	8	9	10
11	12	13	14	15	16	17
18	19	20	21	22	23	24
25	26	27	28	29	30	

June is the sixth month. There are twelve months in a year.

more

There are more ○ than ■.

more likely

It is more likely that I will choose a black button than a white button if I choose a button without looking.

Glossary (Continued)

multiply

$3 \times 5 = 15$

5 + 5 + 5
3 fives

mystery addition

$$28 + \boxed{} = 43$$

$$43 = \boxed{} + 28$$

Find the unknown addend.

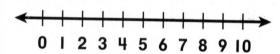

N

New Groups Above Method

$$\begin{array}{r} {\scriptstyle 1} \\ 56 \\ + 28 \\ \hline 84 \end{array}$$

6 + 8 = 14
The 1 new ten in 14 goes up to the tens place.

New Groups Below Method

$$\begin{array}{r} 56 \\ + 28 \\ \hline {\scriptstyle 1} \\ 84 \end{array}$$

6 + 8 = 14
The 1 new ten in 14 goes below in the tens place.

nickel

front   back

5 cents or 5¢ or $0.05

non-standard unit

The length of the pencil is 5 paper clips.

A paper clip is a non-standard unit of length. An inch and a centimeter are standard units of length.

not equal to

$6 + 4 \neq 8$

6 + 4 is not equal to 8.

number line

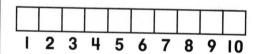

0 1 2 3 4 5 6 7 8 9 10

This is a number line.

number path

| 1 | 2 | 3 | 4 | 5 | 6 | 7 | 8 | 9 | 10 |

This is a number path.

numerator

$\dfrac{3}{4}$ ← numerator

$$\frac{3}{4} = \frac{1}{4} + \frac{1}{4} + \frac{1}{4}$$

The numerator tells how many unit fractions.

odd number

A number is odd if you can make groups of 2 and have one left over.

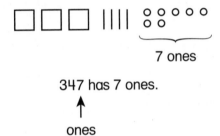

9 is an odd number.

ones

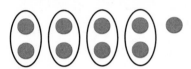

7 ones

347 has 7 ones.
↑
ones

opposite sides

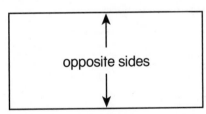

order

The numbers 2, 5, and 6 are in order from least to greatest.

ordinal number

Ordinal numbers name positions.

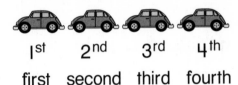

1st   2nd   3rd   4th

first second third fourth

parallel

Lines or line segments that are always the same distance apart.

parallelogram

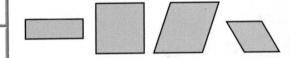

A parallelogram has 2 pairs of parallel sides.

Partner House

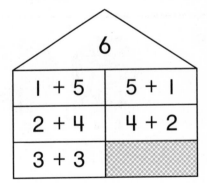

6	
1 + 5	5 + 1
2 + 4	4 + 2
3 + 3	

Glossary (Continued)

partner lengths

partner lengths of 4 cm

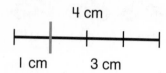

partners

$$9 + 6 = 15$$

↑ ↑
partners

addends

pattern

2, 4, 6, 8, 10, 12

These are patterns.

penny

front   back

1 cent or 1¢ or $0.01

perimeter

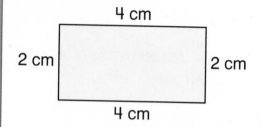

4 cm

2 cm   2 cm

4 cm

perimeter = 2 cm + 4 cm + 2 cm + 4 cm = 12 cm
Perimeter is the total length of the sides.

pictograph

Apples **B**ought

Red	🍎 🍎 🍎 🍎
Green	🍎 🍎
Yellow	🍎 🍎

Key: Each 🍎 stands for 2 apples.

picture graph

Flowers	🌸 🌸 🌸 🌸 🌸 🌸
Vases	🏺 🏺 🏺 🏺 🏺 🏺 🏺 🏺

pie graph

Animals at Grasslands Nature Park

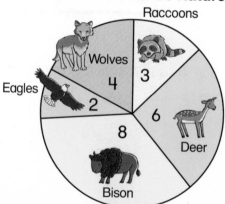

same as a circle graph

plus

$$3 + 2 = 5$$

3 plus 2 equals 5.

$$\begin{array}{r} 3 \\ + 2 \\ \hline 5 \end{array}$$

P.M.

The hours between noon and midnight.

polygons

Polygons have sides that are line segments.

possible

It is possible to choose a white button.
It is possible to choose a black button.

predict

I think it will rain tomorrow.

I predict that it will rain tomorrow.

probability

- What is the probability of choosing a white cube?
- It is likely.

Proof Drawing

Proof Drawing

$$86 + 57 = 143$$

pyramids

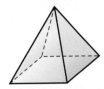

Q

quadrilateral

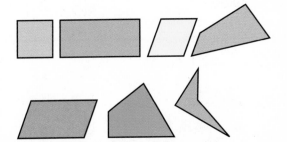

A quadrilateral has 4 sides.

Glossary (Continued)

quarter

front   back

25 cents or 25¢ or $0.25

Quick Hundreds

347

Quick Hundreds

Quick Tens

162

Quick Tens

R

rectangle

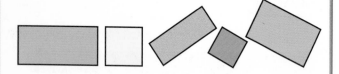

A rectangle has 4 sides and
4 right angles.

rectangular prism

regular polygons

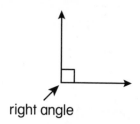

A regular polygon has all sides and all
angles equal.

right angle

right angle

rotation

You can turn or rotate a figure around a point.

round

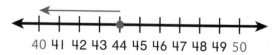

40 41 42 43 44 45 46 47 48 49 50

44 is closer to 40 than 50.
44 rounds to 40.

ruler

A ruler is used to measure length.

scale

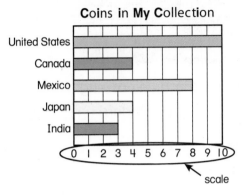

Coins in My Collection

United States
Canada
Mexico
Japan
India

0 1 2 3 4 5 6 7 8 9 10

scale

The numbers along the side or the bottom of a graph.

sequence

Sequences follow a pattern.

2, 4, 6, . . .

9, 8, 7, . . .

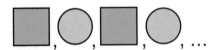

Show All Totals Method

```
  25        724
+ 48      + 158
─────     ─────
  60         12
  13         70
─────       800
  73       ─────
           882
```

similar

These figures are similar. These figures are similar. These figures are not similar.

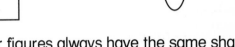

Similar figures always have the same shape and sometimes have the same size.

situation equation

A baker baked 100 loaves of bread. He sold some loaves. There are 73 loaves left. How many loaves of bread did he sell?

$$100 - \boxed{} = 73$$

situation equation

skip count

skip count by 2s: 2, 4, 6, 8, . . .
skip count by 5s: 5, 10, 15, 20, . . .

slide

You can slide a figure right or left along a straight line.

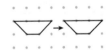

You can slide a figure up or down along a straight line.

Glossary (Continued)

solution equation

A baker baked 100 loaves of bread. He sold some loaves. There are 73 loaves left. How many loaves of bread did he sell?

$100 - 73 = \boxed{}$

$\underbrace{}$

solution equation

sphere

square

A square has 4 equal sides and 4 right angles.

square centimeter

Each side measures 1 centimeter.

1 square centimeter

square unit

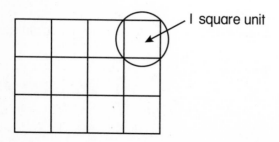

1 square unit

The area of this rectangle is 12 square units.

standard unit

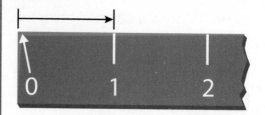

An inch is a standard unit of length.
A paper clip is a non-standard unit of length.

subtract

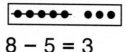

$8 - 5 = 3$

sum

$4 + 3 = 7$

$$\begin{array}{r} 4 \\ +\ 3 \\ \hline 7 \end{array}$$

sum $\longrightarrow$

survey

To collect data by asking people questions.

switch the partners

Show partners in a different order.

$6 + 4 = 10$ $4 + 6 = 10$

partners   partners

symmetry

A figure has symmetry if it can be folded along a line so that the two halves match exactly.

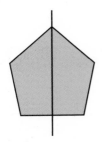

table

	Hamsters	Mice
Kendra	5	8
Scott	2	9
Ida	7	3

tally chart

Favorite Color	Tally Marks	Number of Students
red	||||	4
blue	|||| |	6
yellow	|||| ||	7

teen number

any number from 11 to 19

11 12 13 14 15 16 17 18 19

temperature

A thermometer measures the temperature.

tens

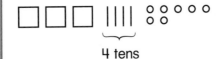

4 tens

347 has 4 tens.

↑

tens

third

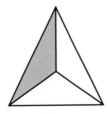

$\frac{1}{3}$ (one third) of the triangle is shaded.

1 of 3 equal parts.

thousand

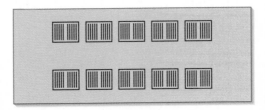

1,000 = ten hundreds

Glossary (Continued)

time

Time is measured in hours, minutes, seconds, days, weeks, months, and years.

total

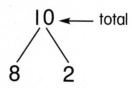

$$10 \leftarrow \text{total}$$

triangle

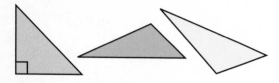

A triangle has 3 sides.

turn

You can **turn** or **rotate** a figure around a point.

twice

Jeremy has twice as many books as Michael.

U

ungroup

$$\begin{array}{c} \overset{0\ \ \ 12}{\cancel{1}}\ \overset{14}{\cancel{3}\,\cancel{4}} \\ -\ \ 7\ 8 \\ \hline 5\ 6 \end{array}$$

Ungroup when you need more ones or tens to subtract.

Ungroup First Method

$$\begin{array}{r} 6\ 4 \\ -\ 2\ 8 \\ \hline \uparrow\ \ \uparrow \\ \text{yes no} \end{array}$$

1. Check to see if there are enough tens and ones to subtract.

$$\begin{array}{r} \overset{5\ \ 14}{\cancel{6}\ \cancel{4}} \\ -\ 2\ 8 \\ \hline \end{array}$$

2. You can get more ones by taking from the tens and putting them in the ones place.

$$\begin{array}{r} \overset{5\ \ 14}{\cancel{6}\ \cancel{4}} \\ -\ 2\ 8 \\ \hline 3\ 6 \end{array}$$

3. Subtract from either right to left or left to right.

unknown

$$3 + \boxed{} = 9 \qquad 3 + 6 = \boxed{}$$

$\uparrow$ unknown partner $\uparrow$ unknown total

V

Venn diagram

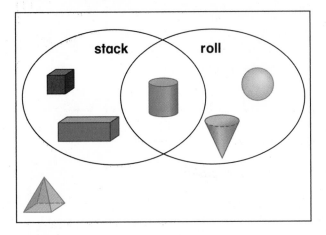

stack   roll

vertex

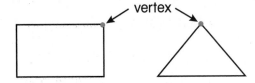

vertex

vertical

$$\begin{array}{r} 4 \\ + 3 \\ \hline 7 \end{array}$$

vertical form   vertical line

view

This is the side view of the rectangular prism above.

volume

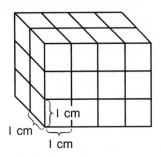

1 cm
1 cm
1 cm

The volume of this rectangular prism is 24 cubic centimeters.

W

weight

2 lb

The weight of this book is 2 pounds.

width

width   or   length
length   width

word name

12

twelve ◀── word name

Y

yard (yd)

3 feet = 1 yard (not drawn to scale)